MORE THAN MATTER?

More than Matter?

*Is There More to Life
Than Molecules?*

Keith Ward

WILLIAM B. EERDMANS PUBLISHING COMPANY
GRAND RAPIDS, MICHIGAN / CAMBRIDGE, U.K.

First published 2010 in the United Kingdom by

Lion Hudson

Wilkinson House, Jordan Hill Road,

Oxford OX2 8DR, England

www.lionhudson.com

This edition published 2011 in the United States of America by

Wm. B. Eerdmans Publishing Co.

2140 Oak Industrial Drive N.E., Grand Rapids, Michigan 49505 /

P.O. Box 163, Cambridge CB3 9PU U.K.

www.eerdmans.com

Printed in the United States of America

17 16 15 14 13 12 11   7 6 5 4 3 2 1

Library of Congress Cataloging-in-Publication Data

Ward, Keith, 1950-

More than matter? : is there more to life than molecules? / Keith Ward.

p.   cm.

Includes bibliographical references and index.

ISBN 978-0-8028-6660-8 (pbk. : alk. paper)

1. Life — Religious aspects — Christianity. 2. Meaning (Philosophy) —

Religious aspects — Christianity. I. Title.

BT696.W37 2011

128 — dc22

2010046256

Contents

Introduction

"You, your joys and sorrows, your memories and your ambitions,
your sense of personal identity and free will, are in fact no more than
the behaviour of a vast assembly of nerve-cells and their associated
molecules." (Francis Crick)[1]

This book exists to put a different view. The success of the physical
sciences has led to a quite widely held view among the scientifically
literate that all that exists is matter or some sort of physical stuff.
Human beings are often presented as the accidental results of
millions of genetic copying-mistakes and freak accidents of nature.
Their cherished ideas of value, freedom, and purpose are illusions,
since humans are nothing but the puppets of blind and mechanical
forces of nature, and their consciousness is doomed to inevitable
extinction, having never been more than a by-product of cosmic
processes to which they are completely unimportant.

I believe that this picture of human life is both scientifically
questionable and philosophically naive. Moreover, it undermines
the belief that human beings, with their thoughts, feelings,
ambitions, and moral challenges and ideals, have intrinsic worth,
and that worth lies in their mental lives, not in the behaviour of
their nerve-cells, however complicated. It is this view, justifying a
commitment to the distinctive value of human consciousness and
responsible action, to which the deepest reflection on the nature of
our cosmos points. That is what I hope to show.

The view that prioritizes human thought, feeling, and action
over the behaviour of physical particles is often called **humanism**,
embodying a commitment to human welfare, interpreted as the
fulfilment of the uniquely personal experiences and creative
capacities of humans. In that sense I am a humanist; but I think
humanism requires ontological backing. That is, there must be good

reasons for seeing human experiences and actions as important and human persons as of intrinsic value in a universe like this.

I intend to produce philosophical reasons for such ontological backing, and I find these reasons intellectually compelling. I make little or no reference to religious considerations, based on revelation or religious authority. But I think there is little doubt that many religious believers will find that the arguments I propound have a natural affinity with some religious beliefs about the human soul, and I myself think that some convergence of humanist and religious beliefs will provide the most adequate view of human persons that is available to us.

But I have confined myself to sustained reflection on the nature of being human, trying to point to phenomena that are available to anyone, whatever their religious beliefs or lack of them. The motto of the book is in fact the reversal of the opening quotation from Crick, and it goes like this: you, your joys and sorrows, your memories and your ambitions, your sense of personal identity and free will, are much more than the behaviour of a vast assembly of nerve-cells, and that "more" gives each personal life a significance and value that expresses and points to the ultimate meaning of the universe itself. Human persons are not accidental mistakes in a pointless perambulation of fundamental particles. They are a window into the inner reality, value, and purpose of the cosmos.

Chapter One

Dualism, minds, and bodies: the problem stated

Gilbert Ryle was an important twentieth-century British philosopher who is famous for attacking what he called "the myth of Cartesian dualism", the myth of the "ghost in the machine". This is the "myth" that minds are different from and more than matter. But was Ryle right? And does his attack also undermine (without meaning to) belief in the unique dignity and value of human persons, which is centred on the nature of their inner experiences and responsible actions? Those are the central questions of this book.

Once upon a time, when I was studying philosophy at Oxford, my supervisor was Gilbert Ryle. He was one of Britain's outstanding philosophers in the 1950s and 60s, and I was one of his last pupils. He was also my moral tutor, though he said, "I do not know what a moral tutor is, and I hope I never have to find out." And, as far as I know, he never did.

9

Although not as well known as Wittgenstein these days, Ryle was extremely influential and was a kind of Oxford equivalent of Wittgenstein, holding views about philosophy that were very similar to those of the Cambridge philosopher. In a sense, this is a book about Wittgenstein as much as it is about Ryle – except that people get so emotional about different interpretations of Wittgenstein's gnomic philosophy that I have thought it better only to make rather muted claims in that area. When I was teaching philosophy in Cambridge, Professor Anscombe, who translated and edited Wittgenstein's later work and often discussed it with me, terrified me so much that I have decided that it is safer to leave discussion of Wittgenstein to acknowledged experts like the Oxford philosopher P. M. Hacker. Nevertheless, I believe that much of what I say about Ryle would apply to Wittgenstein, or at least to many popular interpretations of Wittgenstein, as well.

It is worth talking about Ryle because he was a very good and significant twentieth-century philosopher, and because he wrote the classic critique of Descartes' dualism (usually called Cartesian dualism), the view that the mind and the body are two distinct substances. Ryle originated the expression "the ghost in the machine" to describe Descartes' view, implying that the mind is a ghost (an illusion, really) wandering in the machine of the body. I strongly object to this description, though it has been very influential, and want to try to rehabilitate Descartes, at least to some extent. I want to suggest that mind and consciousness are different from, something over and above, molecules and matter, and that they are not at all ghostly. And I will argue that having such a belief is important if you put a great value on individual human experience and responsible moral action.

Ryle is particularly interesting because he rejected dualism, but he was still a humanist. He thought that you could defend human uniqueness, freedom, and responsibility without having a belief that minds are something more than matter. I do not think this is true, but examining Ryle's arguments is a good way of finding out what you really think about this issue. In fact, it will take me some time to get around to considering Ryle in detail, as there are problems that have to be cleared up first about the nature of philosophy and about differing philosophical views of the nature of reality. I will use the word "metaphysics" to mean a general view about what kinds of things are real (whether, for instance, there are minds in addition to bodies, and whether everything is determined by laws of nature or whether the will is free). Ryle had one such philosophical view, but, oddly enough, he did not think that he had.

He was certainly not a materialist, a person who thinks that everything that exists, including minds, is purely physical, so that minds are "nothing but matter". Nevertheless, his rejection of mind as a distinct substance suggests that, if you are going to have a grand metaphysical theory about what kinds of things exist, you will probably end up as some sort of materialist. And his rejection of materialism has come to seem rather implausible to philosophers like Daniel Dennett, who, as a pupil of Ryle roughly contemporary with me, is a more overt materialist. That is partly because Ryle objected to having any metaphysical theory at all and argued that such grand theories are the results of "logical howlers" or grammatical mistakes. His aim in his best-known book, *The Concept of Mind*, was to correct these mistakes, and rid us of the temptation to think that we could sit in an armchair, philosophize, and thereby discover the nature of reality.

In my case, he completely failed. Despite the worst (or best) he could do, I went on having metaphysical thoughts. I am still having them. I think that there is a major intellectual battle going on, especially in the West, between those who adopt a purely materialist view of human persons and those who believe that there is a distinctive reality and value about human minds, and that such minds far transcend their physical embodiments both in their nature and in their moral worth. This battle is not about a set of grammatical mistakes. It is about what it means to be human and about the distinctive importance of human personhood in our physical universe. It is a metaphysical battle, a battle about what sorts of things exist and about whether persons are distinctive

11

sorts of things that are different from purely material things. This metaphysical battle is real.

Ryle did not hold the fact that I thought this against me. He published my first philosophical article and helped to get me my first philosophical job, in the Logic department at the University of Glasgow. I think he regarded me as a somewhat retarded example of his own early philosophical errors, and expected that I would grow out of them in time. But things have only got worse. I am more than ever convinced that the question of what it is to be a human person is the biggest intellectual question of our day.

Gilbert Ryle and common sense

Philosophy has a job to do. That job is not to provide universally agreed and incontestable answers. It is to examine questions like that of the nature of personhood as deeply as possible, taking account of many different disciplines and points of view. It may help individuals to come to an informed opinion of their own. More likely, it will help to confirm the opinion they already have – but their opinion will be more informed, more aware of its own limitations and weaknesses, and more appreciative of why other opinions exist, and of why it is so difficult to find any agreed position.

Gilbert Ryle made a major contribution to the examination of this question of what it is to be a human person, and whatever he said about metaphysics, he believed that philosophical enquiry was essential for clearing away confusions and needless obscurities. For that reason, as well as out of a sense of relief that he never had to find out what a moral tutor was, I have always valued my discussions with Ryle and have always seen him as one of my philosophical mentors. One of my prized possessions is a signed copy of *The Concept of Mind*. It was not a book I ever agreed with. My whole being rebelled against it from the first. But it was beautifully written. It had the peculiar property that while I was reading it I believed it. Only when I stopped reading did I know that it was wrong, but I could never quite formulate just what was wrong with it.

That, I suppose is the mark of good philosophers. They can make you believe that something is supremely reasonable for the space of half an hour, as they take you into their thought world. But, as David Hume used to say, if you put their books down and go and play backgammon, you quickly recover the ordinary beliefs you had before you read their books and wonder what came over you to make you think what they said was so reasonable.

This is a philosophy book (though I have avoided the lengthy technical discussions that are the mark and pride of the best modern philosophical work), so if it is any good it may have the same effect – it will seem convincing until you put it down, but perhaps not for much longer. I feel just the same about my own books, so it follows that I am pretty sceptical about my own philosophical conclusions. But I have to say that I am not as sceptical about my conclusions as I am about other people's conclusions, and especially about some of Gilbert Ryle's conclusions.

That is because Ryle thinks his conclusions are just ordinary common-sense conclusions, as opposed to the incoherent myth of Cartesian dualism. But I think Ryle's conclusions are not at all commonsensical. In fact, they contradict many common-sense beliefs about human persons, their minds, and their bodies.

What are these common-sense beliefs about human beings? That we are physical objects in space and time, animals that are born and die, quite quickly wearing out and decaying like most physical objects. Unlike many physical objects, we perceive, think, feel, and act to achieve goals. We have a mental life.

Nobody else, not even our closest friends, we often think, really appreciates how we feel. It often seems to us that we are constantly misunderstood and under-appreciated, and nobody else ever really knows what it is like to be us.

Further, by dint of heroic personal struggles, we make major contributions to the world. These, too, are rarely appreciated by others, who are all too ready to accuse us of dishonesty or selfishness, when we have only been trying to make the best of a very complex situation and improve life for everybody. Or that is what we all tend to think.

We also have very complicated relations with other people. They teach us our language and skills, but they often try to use or abuse us, and we have to choose our friends very carefully so that we can make our way in a largely hostile and untrustworthy world. Many secret plots and subterfuges are required if we are to acquire a position of status and authority, and if possible – it seems these days – become a celebrity whom everyone admires and imitates.

If we put all these rather gloomy and absurdly self-regarding but common-sense thoughts into philosophical language, we can say that humans have unique memories, thoughts, and feelings to which no one else has complete access. They have the power to act intentionally to achieve various purposes. And they interact with other persons who are also intentional agents with hidden feelings of their own, who are parts of a social culture which shapes the thoughts, feelings, and skills of each individual member of that culture.

I think that Ryle's picture of human persons in *The Concept of Mind* fails to give an adequate account of this mental life of human beings, and gives an unduly vague and incomplete account of responsible human action. However, it gives a rather good account of the social reality of persons. So it only partly fits our common-sense beliefs about human persons. And, regrettably, it has helped to demonize Descartes in recent philosophy by putting Descartes' views in a very distorted way. I still love Ryle's book and am immensely indebted to him as a teacher and philosophical role model. For a while I even smoked a pipe, as he did, thinking that this was part of being a proper philosopher. But as I grew older I gave up smoking and decided that I really preferred the views that Ryle himself had before he complicated his early common sense with anti-Cartesian philosophy and excessive pipe-smoking.

The Cartesian myth: the ghost in the machine

What about "Descartes' Myth", as Ryle terms it in chapter one of his book? It states, according to Ryle, that "minds are not in space".[1] Further, "only I can take direct cognisance of the states... of my own mind". And "of at least some of these episodes he [the person whose mental states they are] has direct and unchallengeable cognisance".[2]

The thing is that I regard these as plain facts, not myths. Thoughts, feelings, sense-perceptions, mental images, dreams, recalled memories, and intentions, cannot be observed at any location in public space. The temptation these days is to say that they are in the brain. It is of course true that if the brain is not working properly, thoughts or images will not occur. But even if my brain is scanned, observers of the scan can only register the occurrence of electrical activity or enhanced blood flow in a region of my brain. They cannot observe the thought or image I am having. They cannot be directly aware of it in the way that I am.

The obvious thing to say is that thoughts can only occur in humans if brain activity occurs, and that thoughts are correlated in some way with specific sorts of brain activity. But the content of a thought – what it is about – cannot be detected by observation of physical activity in my brain. It can, however, be detected by me, though obviously not by observing my own brain and not by observing any portion of physical space.

Each of us can detect the content of a thought without observing it in space, and in a way in which no one else can detect it. It does not follow that my detection is "unchallengeable", though usually we would give an introspective report of what someone is thinking a higher authority than an observer's report of what that person is thinking. But I guess that introspective reports are as fallible as most reports. That is, they are likely to be correct in general, but not always, especially under very unusual or complex conditions (like being in a brain-scanner).

So far, as far as I am concerned, the myth is not a myth at all, but a statement of what is apprehended to be the case. Did Ryle really think that other people could observe what he was thinking when he sat in his chair smoking his pipe and frowning slightly? I at least had to wait until he spoke, and even then I wasn't always sure what he had just thought. Perhaps he wasn't sure either, but he was surely in a better position than I was to say what he was thinking. He had privileged access by introspection to his own thoughts, even when he was thinking that there was no such thing as introspection or privileged access. Yet that, it seemed to me, was a self-refuting thought to think!

Logical positivism and other people

When, after talking to Ryle for an hour, I began to wonder whether anyone had any private experiences, I would take a short walk from Magdalen College to New College to visit Professor Ayer, also in Oxford at that time, and be reassured that he at least had private experiences (which he called "sense-data"). In fact, he had hardly anything but sense-data.

Ayer was a logical positivist, which meant that he thought all factual assertions had to be verifiable by some sense-experience. Ayer had a very rigorous definition of what a sense-experience (a sense-datum) was. It had to be an immediate datum of some sense (sight, hearing, smell, taste or touch), without including any inferences or theories. So a sense-datum is something like a patch of red or a sound or a sudden smell or taste. Positivists thought that all meaningful words must refer to such data in the end, and you could verify the truth of statements by just having the appropriate sense-data. If you could not do that, words and sentences were actually meaningless. This was positivism, because it insisted that all knowledge is analysable into confrontation with bare sense-data (it is "positive", as opposed to speculative or theoretical). It was logical, because it told you what words were meaningful, and what words were not.

A funny thing about sense-data is that they seem to be essentially private. Nobody else can have my sense-data, and I cannot have theirs. In fact, persons are nothing but chains of sense-data, and these chains can never overlap or meet. So when Ayer met other people, what was really happening was that his chain of sense-data included sounds, smells, and sights that looked like the bodies of other people. But they were really just sets of sense-data, and the theory that they were other people was just a theory, a sort of shorthand to make things more convenient (so it is not really so "positive" or non-theoretical after all!). The existence of an objective physical world with other people in it was, Ayer thought, a construction out of sense-data.

As a good logical positivist, Ayer believed that he constructed the whole world, including physical objects and other people, out of his own private experiences. Following this thought through to its logical conclusion, it followed that all the students in his seminars were actually constructed out of parts of Professor Ayer. This was even more disconcerting, however, than Ryle's denial that Ayer was having any private experiences, so I felt the truth must lie somewhere in between these two completely conflicting views of two of the most eminent philosophers in Britain at the time.

What did Ryle have against private experiences? I think that he feared that once he got into a world of private experiences, he would never get out again. Each person would be locked into their own little private world, with no way of communicating with, or even of knowing what was going on in, any other person's little private world. "Absolute solitude is on this showing the ineluctable destiny of the soul. Only our bodies can meet," he said.[3]

He felt that, in a dualist view, minds and bodies would be two completely separate sorts of thing. Since each mind is essentially private, the best we could do would be to infer unobservable mental events from people's bodily movements. But we could never check whether our inferences were correct. We could never be sure anything was going on in the minds of other people at all. And we could never say what sort of transaction was taking place between minds and bodies, since such transactions between two such different realms would belong neither to bodies nor to minds. They would be forever mysterious and beyond reasonable explanation.

On a Cartesian view, the gulf between mind and body is so wide, Ryle thought, that when we make a remark about someone's thoughts or intentions, "the onlooker... can never assure himself that his comments have any vestige of truth".[4] Bodily behaviour might be wholly disconnected from the inner mental events which are forever hidden from others: "External observers could never know how the overt behaviour of others is correlated with their mental powers."[5]

This is indeed a puzzle that philosophy teachers like to place before first-year undergraduates. If all our knowledge begins from our own experience, how can we ever be sure that anything exists beyond our experience? How do we know that our best friends are not robots, without real minds? How do we know that we are not being totally deceived in thinking there really are any other people with thoughts and feelings?

This could be called the "Matrix" problem (from the film of that name). Might we not all be in some gigantic factory, wired up to machines that produce in our brains the illusion that we are talking to other people, while the truth is that some machine is producing sets of false beliefs in us? There are actually no other people there, just bodies that act and speak as if they were people. And in that case, even the bodies are illusions, so we really are in trouble.

The irony is that this is exactly the sort of problem Descartes was trying to deal with, as he asked himself what he could be absolutely certain of, without any possibility of doubt. But whereas Descartes thought the thing we could be most certain of was our minds, Ryle claimed that we did not have any minds (in this sense) at all. If we did have minds, we would have all the insuperable problems just outlined. What I want to ask is whether this is really true. I am pretty sure that it is not.

The Dead Philosophers' Club

In some obscure corner of limbo we might imagine the Dead Philosophers' Club meeting regularly to discuss whether they had ever really existed. (Or we could have imagined this before Pope Benedict XVI officially abolished limbo.) Now the members of the club have even more reason to suspect that they do not really exist, as their accustomed meeting place has disappeared, by papal command.

Nevertheless, we might imagine Professor Ayer meeting up with Gilbert Ryle to discuss deep problems of philosophy, including the major problem of whether they were talking to each other at all.

"Ryle, I wish you would stop smoking that pipe," Ayer might say. "Don't you know that smoking is very bad for your health?"

Ryle could reply, "Being dead is not very good for your health either, but I have to put up with it. In any case your cigarettes are much worse than my pipe."

"That," Ayer might say, "is just your subjective opinion. Since subjective expressions of opinion have no truth-value, it follows that it is not true."

"Is it not just your subjective opinion that I am sitting here smoking my pipe?"

"Not at all. That is a fact. Statements about facts have a truth-value, and my experience can verify their truth, if they are true. I am quite certain that you are smoking your pipe or at least that someone very like you is smoking something very like a pipe. Admittedly my evidence is not as conclusive as I would like, and you could, after all, be just a set of visual sense-data that give me a strong impression that it is you who is sitting there. I suppose what I am really certain of is that a set of coloured shapes

exists in my visual field; but they look remarkably like Gilbert Ryle to me."

"That is a very odd thing to be certain of. I, on the other hand, am quite certain that there are no such things as sense-data, so you can hardly be certain that you are having some of them. That would be to fall into a gross Cartesian error."

"We both agree, Ryle, that whatever else is the case, Descartes fell into a gross error. But we seem to disagree about what the error was. You seem to think he was mistaken in thinking there were any private thoughts. I am sure that there are private thoughts, but I think he was mistaken in thinking that anybody was thinking them. Perhaps, though, we can both agree that he was mistaken in thinking that the mind is an immaterial thing which is churning out thoughts, whereas we know that there is no such thing, no ghost of Descartes hidden in the machine which is his body."

And there we might leave the Dead Philosophers' Club, with two of its leading members being absolutely certain of totally different things, and being equally certain that the other is wrong. Furthermore, there does not seem to be any way of deciding who is correct, which means that they can go on discussing the issue forever, without ever being in danger of coming to an agreed conclusion. I rather think that this should at least make philosophers relatively modest in their claims and open to the possibility of reasonable disagreement. It may even be quite an intellectual advance to recognize the tentative nature of human guesses about the ultimate nature of reality, and the impossibility of arriving at complete agreement about it. At the very least, we will not be able to regard all those who disagree with us as fools and knaves – though no doubt some of them are (I'm not saying who).

Chapter Two

A range of philosophical views about what is really real

Dualism – the view that mind or spirit is different from body and brain – is widely derided in much modern thought. But actually it is just one of a number of widely held philosophical views about what is really real, and about what human persons are. In this chapter I outline five of them, all held by reputable philosophers: phenomenalism (the view that all human knowledge is built up from, and is basically limited to, sense-experience); naive realism (the view that the world exists very much as we see it, even when we are not observing it); materialism (the view that only material objects, perhaps publicly observable objects in space-time, are ultimately real); dualism; and epiphenomenalism (the view that minds exist and are different from matter, but that they are wholly dependent upon brains, and play no causal role in anything that happens, as the material brain does all the work). Materialism, though currently very popular, is just one of these views, and I argue

*that on purely philosophical grounds materialism is
less plausible than dualism.*

What is really real? Are there sense-data, as Ayer supposed? Is there
an immaterial thinker, as Descartes supposed? Or are (almost) all
statements about minds analysable into dispositional, "if-then"
statements about the behaviour of publicly observable bodies, as
Ryle supposed? It seems as if what these philosophers are doing is
to start from a basic set of axioms, trace out what can be inferred
or deduced from them, and then see how these consequences
fit with their experience of reality. They are each able to see the
weaknesses in their opponents' theories, and propose accounts
that try to remedy them. Ayer accepts Descartes' claim that mental
occurrences like thoughts and images could exist without physical
bodies, but rejects the claim that there is an immaterial subject
who has such thoughts and images. Ryle accepts Ayer's claim that
all factual statements must be verifiable in principle, but rejects
the claim that such verification consists in having private sense-
experiences which no one else could ever check. I am accepting
Ryle's claim that many (not all) statements about mental properties
are dispositional statements about what a human animal is capable
of doing or is liable to do in various circumstances. But I am
querying his claim that there are no private and non-spatially
locatable mental occurrences.

Does this mean there is a ghost in the machine after all? Ghosts
are usually visual appearances of people, but they lack solidity and
they tend to moan and wail rather a lot. I don't suppose anyone
thinks that inside their head there is a wailing gaseous hallucination
which pulls the levers that make the brain work. That is plainly
ridiculous, and it is meant to be. The metaphor of a ghost in the
machine has worked well as a rhetorical device to make people
think that we all know the brain (the machine) is real, whereas talk
of a mind other than the brain or of mental events in addition to

brain-events is talk about something peculiar, not quite real, and probably illusory (a ghost).

It seems to me that the situation is quite the reverse. Talk of mental events is the most real thing we humans know. We know we have sense-experiences, bodily sensations, thoughts, feelings, and images. We know we experience things in ways that are unique to us and never wholly communicable to other people. We know that all our knowledge of the world has to begin with such experiences. Mental events are real, and to deny them would deprive us of all knowledge. They are not ghosts or hallucinations at all.

But do we know that brains are real? Well, yes, because we can see and feel them, at least if we are surgeons or pathologists. But may the brains we observe only be appearances to us of a reality which is rather different from what we see? This is another standard problem for first-year philosophers: what would brains look like if we were not looking at them?

We can never find out by observation, because every time we look at something we only see the way it looks to us. It is no use trying to cheat by closing our eyes and then opening them very quickly, as if to take the world by surprise. However quickly and surprisingly we manage to take a peek, we still only see what things look like to us. We can never manage to take them unawares, and find out what they look like when no one is looking at them.

This is very frustrating. We are tempted to say, "Well, obviously, they go on being the same whether we are looking at them or not." But there are good reasons for thinking this is not true. One of the most important features of objects in our experience is colour. When we admire a beautiful view, we usually admire the colours objects have. But physicists tell us that colour is a product of the brain. External objects emit electromagnetic waves. Some of these impinge on the cones in human eyes, and cause electrochemical impulses that land up in the visual cortex. Only after that long causal journey do colours appear to us. The original wavelengths have no colour. They cause sensations of colour when they affect human sense-organs and the human brain. Colours are precisely some of those private mental states that Ryle wanted to get rid of. Different individuals may see colours in rather different ways. Colour-blind people certainly do. And some animals do not seem to see colours at all (they have no cones in their eyes). What we see depends on our cognitive apparatus.

But where are the colours themselves? They are not literally in the brain, as physical objects. The brain does not change colour when we see coloured objects. They are not on the objects we see, which have no colour. Colours are, as John Locke said, following Galileo, secondary qualities. They do not belong to external objects. They are contents of the mind, when stimulated by the brain, which in turn has been stimulated by wavelengths of light. Colours are caused by physical events, but they are not themselves physical events. They are how consciousness perceives physical events. There is a causal basis of conscious events, but it does not exist as we see it.

Brains are rather boring, where colour is concerned. They are usually greyish. But are brains grey when we are not looking at them? Apparently not; they then have no colour at all. In fact, we could go much further than this and say that brains are not the solid porridge-looking objects they appear to be. Any physicist will say that brains are mostly empty space, in which molecules, atoms, electrons, quarks, and other strange particles buzz about in complicated ways.

It seems as though physical objects, when not being observed, have no colours, and no sounds, smells or tastes either. Sounds, like colours, are not physical events. Neither are smells, tastes or sensations. Things do not smell like, taste like or feel like anything, when nobody is smelling, tasting or feeling them. The physical world, it seems, is totally vacuous. No colours, sounds, smells, tastes or sensations. What on earth is left?

Wet philosophers

For Locke and Galileo, what is left is a world of "primary qualities" – qualities which, they thought (wrongly, as modern physics shows) physical objects cannot fail to have, but which are quite distinct from the "secondary qualities" that we see, hear, and feel, but which do not belong to the physical world. The world of primary qualities, the "real world", is basically a world of colourless, intangible, inaudible particles located in space, moving around and continually bumping into one another (though of course not realizing that they are doing so).

Science tells us that all objects are made of atoms and other very small particles, and that atoms have no colour, smell or taste. They just have properties like mass, charge, position, and momentum. So they are not exactly how they look to a human being.

When oxygen and hydrogen atoms are put together in a particular way, they feel wet to human observers – they form molecules of water. But if there were no observers, they would not be wet. There would not be any wetness. There would only be what John Stuart Mill called "a permanent possibility" of wetness, which would only become actually wet when somebody went for a swim.

Thus there is no point in asking Mill whether the sea is warm enough for swimming. He would have to reply, "Not yet, but it might be if you jump in." Anyone who thinks that we see things as they actually are, however, would say that the sea is wet and warm, even if there is nobody about. But there is a problem. How do we know? There is absolutely no way of checking, without jumping in – and then of course you have not proved that it was wet and warm before you jumped in. This is why, on the philosophers' annual outing to the seaside, you may observe groups of philosophers rapidly jumping in and out of the sea, to try to see whether it remains wet or not. But they can never be sure it is going to be wet before they jump in, and they can never prove that it is still wet after they jump out.

We might say that it is just common sense to say that the sea continues to be wet when there is no one in it. But it must be admitted that it cannot be proved by sense-experience or observation. It is just much simpler to say that if the sea is wet every time you jump in, it is wet in between jumps. Of course that hypothesis will not work if you only jump in the sea once a year. But if you jump in and out as quickly as possible, it is the simplest explanatory hypothesis to account for why we can more or less predict that the sea is going to be wet.

So we can assume that the sea continues to be wet even when there is nobody in it. Nevertheless, it is probably safer, even if a little more complicated, to say that the sea is such that, if we jump into it, we will find it wet. There is some continuing causal basis for our feelings of wetness, though there is no actual unobserved wetness in the sea. That is what Galileo, John Locke, and John Stuart Mill, all supposed.

Weird science

Bishop Berkeley famously objected to any distinction between primary and secondary qualities. He held, with some justification, that talk about tiny colourless atoms bouncing about is a mere abstraction. Why should we think that such abstractions are real, when in fact this world we observe, with all its smells, tastes, and colours, is the most real thing we know? There is little reason to suppose that science tells us the truth about reality, whereas the senses only provide appearances. It would make more sense to suppose that both science and common sense are concerned with appearances produced by the interaction of a hidden reality with human minds.

Though Bishop Berkeley has become a by-word for silliness among many philosophers, there are things in modern physics that give him some support. The so-called "real world" posited by classical Newtonian science is not only an abstraction. It has passed its sell-by date, and it is nowhere near abstract enough. For quantum science, the world has dissolved into sets of probability waves in Hilbert space, of entangled and superposed wave-particles, and of ten- or twenty-six-dimensional curved space-time manifolds, which probably arise by quantum fluctuations in a vacuum. If you want something abstract, try that on for size.

This scientific view of the real world is about as far from what most people believe, or could even imagine, as it is possible to get. Common-sense consciousness, which is the sort most common people have, experiences things as colourful, tasty, smelly, and wet. Why should we think that the scientific world of probability waves and so on is the real world, as it is in itself when it is not being observed, whereas the common-sense world is just that world as it appears to us?

There is a great deal of controversy about the interpretation of fundamental physics. Some theorists, like Michio Kaku of the City College of New York, one of the founders of string field theory, boldly claim that "the matter in the universe and the forces that hold it together... may be nothing but different vibrations of hyperspace".[1] Superstrings require a ten- or twenty-six-dimensional universe, and the basic forces of electromagnetism, gravity, and the nuclear forces may be caused by the "crumpling" of a universe that exists in dimensions far beyond the four-dimensional space-time of our common-sense observations (not that common sense usually gets even as far as four dimensions).

Other physicists, like Niels Bohr, prefer to think that the world of observation is fundamentally real, and that all talk of such things as hyperspace uses mathematical constructs that cannot be mapped onto any objectively existing reality. In other words, quantum field theory does not tell us what the objective world is "really" like. As Bishop Berkeley suggested, we cannot get beyond a world of appearances, of things-as-they-appear-to-us, whether they appear as sense-perceptions or as mathematical intelligible mental constructions.

After all, probability waves are not actual waves. They are mathematical devices for assigning probabilities to discovering the location of an electron under specific constraining conditions of measurement. You might say that electrons are probably in a number of places at the same time, but they are not actually at any precise place. That is certainly not common sense, and it is very hard to believe. Quantum physics is undoubtedly correct. Its predictions have been verified many times. Yet equally undoubtedly it does not give an adequate description of how things really are. It provides a set of sophisticated mathematical operations for understanding the behaviour of very small energy interactions under controlled and relatively isolated conditions. But one could not say that the variables of the formulae correspond to so-called "real entities". They are constructions of the mind.

The conclusion, for a number of quantum physicists, is not that there is really nothing there at all. It is that reality is hidden from us in its inner nature. All we can do is construct hypotheses that explain the structure of its interactions with our minds. But if we consider that our minds play a fundamental role in constructing both the sensory world that the senses reveal and the mathematical world that the mind explores, we may be led to the opinion that mind or consciousness is a foundational element of reality. As the eminent quantum theorist John von Neumann put it, "All real things are contents of consciousness." Bishop Berkeley lives again, as the solid Newtonian world of classical physics dissolves into the abstract mathematical world of quantum theory, and leaves the mind as the most "solid" and basic constituent of the real world.

It is time to pause and take stock. We have already come across three main philosophical opinions about what the world we experience is really like.

First, there is the opinion that the things we perceive are just what they seem to be – warm, wet, fuzzy, and colourful (they might also be beautiful or ugly, ordered or chaotic, pleasant or unpleasant, though that is disputed). The world of sense-experience is the real world.

Second, there is the opinion that our senses disclose only appearances or things as they appear to us. In itself reality is very different, and science and intellectual reflection can tell us what it is like. The world of science is the real world.

Third, there is the opinion that appearance and reality are indeed different. But fundamental science deals in abstract mathematical constructions, and such abstractions do not tell us what reality in itself is like. We do not know what the real world is like. But both sense-experience and science are constructions of the mind, so maybe hidden reality is something like consciousness or mind.

These three philosophical positions, which are basic metaphysical theories (theories about what sorts of things really exist, and what sorts of things are actually real, not just apparent), can be, have been, and still are, ably defended by philosophers. My own preference is for some form of the third view, and I shall try to defend it. The discomfort I feel with Ryle's philosophy is that it seems to espouse some form of the first view, and this basic (and in my view mistaken) commitment is presupposed in all his specific arguments about the concept of mind. If the third view is right, things will look very different, as I shall show.

What you see is what you get

On closer inspection, the three main views I have outlined split into many further into subdivisions. I will restrain myself and mention only a total of eight philosophical possibilities. No doubt we could think of even more divisions and different kinds of overlap between views – there is probably one sub-division for every philosopher who has ever lived – but eight is enough to be going on with.

The reason why it is important to examine these metaphysical views is that the problem of what persons really are cannot be resolved unless we have first come to a decision about what sorts of things fundamentally exist. Many discussions about the nature of persons fail to tackle this more fundamental question or even fail to see that it is a really difficult problem. Many people just assume some sort of common-sense view, that humans are evolved animals in space and time, and that this three-dimensional world that we experience is what is actually real. Other people, more scientifically inclined perhaps, admit that the real world is very different from the one we see and feel, but it is still definitely and completely material. There are no "spooky" or "supernatural" entities, and Cartesian dualism, in particular, is just a relic of an outmoded superstition.

If we are going to approach the issue rationally, however, we need to see that these are just two out of a pretty large field of possible metaphysical options. In fact, they are both very controversial and highly contested from a philosophical point of view. It is only when we see the wider range of metaphysical options that we realize how tenuous the arguments for common sense and for materialism are.

I am going to argue that the most adequate view of human persons will fall under what I have called the third group of metaphysical theories, which says that there is a reality underlying our everyday experience whose basic character is consciousness or mind. So I need to establish that this is a coherent and plausible metaphysical view. That means setting it out alongside some other major metaphysical views, and showing their strengths and weaknesses. That is what I am now going to do.

The first group of metaphysical theories is the "things are basically what they seem to the senses to be" group. The most radical version of this is the view that when nobody is observing things, when they are not contents of consciousness, there is nothing there. There is only what David Hume calls a succession of impressions and ideas. The idea of a continuing unobserved world is a postulate of the imagination, and, if we were trying to get the simplest possible account of the world, such a postulate would be regarded as superfluous. Things are what they seem to be, but there is no objective continuing world to support the things we see, hear, and touch. If we attend closely to what we experience, we will realize that we never experience unobserved continuing physical objects. So there aren't any such things.

This extreme position – a sort of radical empiricism, sometimes called **phenomenalism** (I will call it Theory 1) – is too much for most people, but it makes the point that the common-sense belief that there is a world of physical objects depends upon rational postulates that, strictly speaking, cannot be substantiated simply by appeal to experience. Most people do make such postulates and accept a philosophy of common sense. They assume that things continue to be roughly what they are observed to be even when nobody is observing them. We live in a real world of objects in three-dimensional space, and we observe it more or less as it is (this is Theory 2, sometimes called **naive realism**, because many philosophers think it really is rather naive).

I think the consideration of properties like colours is sufficient to render this view improbable, especially since we can carry out the same type of analysis for smells, tastes, sensations, and sounds. Nevertheless, I suspect Ryle holds some version of this opinion. At least he speaks as though he does, though to put it like that possibly sounds too "metaphysical" for his taste. Like Wittgenstein, he would probably think that "everything is in order as it is", that metaphysics raises a host of pseudo-problems that arise from linguistic confusions, and that philosophy can provide no new information about the world, least of all about "ultimate reality". Philosophy has no theories.

The problem is, that is a theory. And Ryle does, as I have suggested, have some beliefs that fly in the face of common sense – for instance, that there are no objects that are not in publicly observable space (the contents of minds, those "ghosts in the machine"). Common sense says that there are dreams, images, sensations, feelings, and thoughts that are not observable in space. At least *my* common sense does, and most people I meet down the pub think it does, and if we are not common, who is? Common sense says that things are what they seem to most people to be, but we do not explore too deeply what happens to things when we are not looking at them.

The people who do explore that sort of thing are physicists. Common sense seems to conflict in a marked way with modern physics. This fact leads into the second group of theories about the nature of the world we experience, that science tells us the truth about reality. Modern physicists sometimes say that there are other space-times ("many worlds" or a **multiverse** of universes), and if so those space-times are certainly not publicly observable in this space.

Space and time are only four of many possible dimensions, and physicists like Stephen Hawking envisage realms of being in which space or time does not exist at all or can become interchangeable. It seems to be an open question whether there are non-spatial entities, and philosophers are not going to avoid it by saying that it arises from a logical mistake or category error.

There's more to life than meets the eye

So we are led beyond common sense toward the currently fashionable position that science tells us about a world that is very uncommonsensical indeed. Because physicists do not like to think of themselves as naive, this is sometimes called critical realism as opposed to naive realism (the unkind term for common sense). The world as it is in itself is not as we observe it in experience. But it has nameable properties such as mass, position, and velocity, and science – preferably fundamental physics – can tell us what they are.

Since the 1930s it has become much more questionable what nameable properties fundamental physics does tell us about. If there is five times as much dark matter in the world as there is matter that we can see, if the fundamental forces of our space-time are in fact crumplings of ten-dimensional hyperspace, and if fields and tensors have replaced particles and waves as the fundamental stuff of the universe, we might well begin to wonder what may be coming next. It sometimes seems that physicists are telling us that something is most definitely real, but we are no longer sure just what it is. This realism is so critical that it seems to have become pretty unrealistic.

This is what I mean by saying that materialism, at least in the sense of saying that everything that exists must have a location and extension in space-time, seems to be scientifically questionable. Many modern physicists have left ordinary space and time well behind. Nevertheless, advances in other scientific areas like neuroscience and artificial intelligence have encouraged a view that all mental events must be identical with spatio-temporally locatable events in the brain. This has led to the adoption of varieties of **materialism** (Theory 3) which presuppose that, whatever some physicists say, the scientific world is the only one that exists, and the scientific world contains only material entities.

There are physicists who would support materialism in a more sophisticated form (sometimes called physicalism or naturalism), extending the idea of matter (or energy) considerably, but insisting that all that exists must be material in that extended sense. For instance, if our subjective sense of time passing is the result of a crumpling of hyperspace, or even if time is a fourth dimension in some realistic sense, then our consciousness of passing through time may not be a good clue to what reality is like. Time may be there "all at once", existing from beginning to end as a fourth dimension, and we just seem to be passing through it. For such views our sense of personal development, of having interesting and unique experiences one after the other, is an illusion, as is consciousness itself. Only the material, as defined by the latest scientific theory, is real.

It is not quite clear, however, who would be having such an illusion. Anyway, illusions seem to have some sort of existence. If I seem to see something, there must be something that I seem to see; there must be a "seeming" as well as a "reality". Or must there?

Headless women

Suppose a conjurer makes it appear that he saws off a woman's head, and in consequence I seem to see a headless woman. That is an illusion – the head is there, but I fail to see it. I do not in fact see a woman without a head. I fail to see the head of the woman. I do not see what I think I see. So it is not true that if I seem to see X, there must be an X that I seem to see. However, there is something that I see. I see a woman whose head is concealed, but I misdescribe what I see. That is easily done. Conjuring tricks work because they are easily done. We often make mistakes when we describe what we see. Yet there is something I see, even though I have the description wrong.

Compare this with "having the illusion" that I am passing through time, one second after another (whereas, in fact, past, present, and future all exist in one four- (or more) dimensional continuum, and I am not moving through time at all). What is it that I seem to see? One thing happening after another. But could I be describing this wrongly? This would be like saying that time is actually all there "at once", but I (wrongly) see it as one thing after another. Even if I am misdescribing it, however, I am seeing one thing after another. Someone (me) is having the experience of a succession of times. So a succession of times does exist – in my experience.

That is enough to establish that my experience has properties that objective time does not – properties of temporal succession. Even if time is an illusion, we must distinguish personal experience from objective physical reality. Therefore it cannot be true that personal experience does not exist. Illusions, too, exist, and have properties that do not belong to objective reality.

The extreme materialist view that consciousness is an illusion can only be consistently held by philosophers who are not conscious. Therefore most conscious philosophers who are dissatisfied with common sense distinguish personal experience from objective reality, and maintain that while subjective conscious experiences do exist, objective (unobserved) reality has whatever properties scientists ascribe to it. This is actually what Cartesian **dualism** (Theory 4), Ryle's main target, maintains. Conscious experiences are distinct from material objects, and you cannot get rid of them simply by saying that they are illusions.

You could, however, say that consciousness somehow "emerges from" complex physical structures like the brain, even if you have no idea how it does so. This has been termed **epiphenomenalism**(Theory 5), since consciousness is regarded as a by-product of the physical brain that does not influence behaviour. Descartes did not think consciousness could emerge from matter, since they are so different from one another, and causes, he thought, can only produce effects like themselves. But you could just say that this need not be the case. If one sort of thing (matter) produces another type of thing (mind), there is no point in complaining that we cannot see how it is done. We just have to live with it.

It should be noted, however, that if you say this, you will also just have to accept that matter, or changes in matter, might be produced by minds. So minds could produce physical changes or even possibly physical entities, and again it would be useless for philosophers to complain that they cannot understand how it happens. They will just have to get over it. Mind–matter interaction might be real.

Nevertheless, scientifically minded philosophers often assert that all genuine causes are physical, whereas the personal or mental is a sort of by-product that plays no effective role in governing what happens in the world. This seems to be just a basic dogma – all causes must be physical, because I say so. (I should add that I am not against having basic dogmas. We all have them, but at least we should acknowledge that they are dogmas, and are by no means obvious to everybody.) It is certainly not an opinion that is confirmed by observation or by any natural science. Of course the dogma is not produced by some arbitrary whim. It is produced by the adoption of an elegant and comprehensive explanatory hypothesis – that the unobserved world has the "primary properties" noted by physical science, but no "secondary properties" which belong only to subjective experience. The hypothesis can become very tightly constraining, when it is postulated that the physical world is governed by a simple set of absolute and inflexible laws which wholly determine everything that happens. This is the "machine world" against which Ryle also inveighs. And in that machine personal experiences or the subjects of such experiences become "ghosts", illusory apparitions with no causal part to play in the workings of the cosmic machine.

The big options

I have now collected five of the eight philosophical views I wanted to outline. Phenomenalism (Theory 1) and naive realism

(Theory 2) attempt to maintain that reality is basically what it seems to be to the human senses. The advance of the natural sciences introduces critical realism, and this in turn subdivides into materialist views that mind is not a thing at all (Theory 3), dualistic views that mind and matter are distinct (Theory 4), and epiphenomenalist views that mind does exist, but is a product of and wholly dependent upon the physical world that science correctly describes (Theory 5).

One reason I have listed these views is to make the point that there are many defensible philosophical opinions about the nature of the world we observe and know, and about our own natures as observers and agents in that world. There is not just one obviously true opinion. In fact my suggestion is that the third group of metaphysical theories, which I am just about to embark on, is more plausible than the first two groups. The three members of the third group could be called forms of idealism, which is, in its most general form, the belief that mind or consciousness is more real than matter or provides a better clue to the nature of reality as a whole. If I could establish that, we would be well on the way to showing that human persons are not just complex bundles of matter and molecules. Their moral importance and value lies crucially in their mental lives and acts.

Of course I do not expect to establish it to everyone's satisfaction. No philosopher ever manages to do such a thing. But I do hope to show that idealism is a coherent and plausible view, fully consistent with the best modern scientific knowledge. And I hope to show that the philosophy of materialism, which is assumed by many to be obviously true, is far from obvious and contains major weaknesses from which idealism is free.

Underlying all this discussion is the belief that metaphysical differences are real and important. Ryle's claim that he is only rectifying the logic of our language about minds[2] by distinguishing logical categories, and not making any statements about the nature of the world, is unconvincing. Ordinary language carries philosophical presuppositions. It presupposes – contrary to what

Ryle claims – that minds are causes on occasion, that humans are at least sometimes free agents, and that private states of consciousness exist. If we ceased to believe these things, our language might well change.

Philosophical reflection can make a difference to what we say, to how we speak, and to what we claim to know. The rise of the natural sciences has raised questions about human personhood in a sharp way. It has given rise to radical forms of dualism, which separate minds and bodies completely, and to materialism, which eliminates minds (in this sense) altogether. So another goal I have in mind is to place radical dualism and materialism in historical context as extreme responses to new scientific knowledge, and to point forward to more adequate interpretations of contemporary knowledge.

This of course is what Ryle thought he was doing. He rejected both radical dualism and materialism as inadequate philosophical theories, and tried to replace them with a more rounded view of humans as essentially social animals. In doing this, he was importantly right. His mistake was to think that he had no philosophical theory, but was only stating the obvious (once people got their logic right). But that, ironically, *was* his philosophical theory.

Chapter Three

The limits of knowledge

Another major philosophical view is idealism: the theory that reality is mind or mind-like, and that material things are appearances of this reality to consciousness. This is the view I aim to defend. Most classical European philosophers have accepted some form of it. It was most fully formulated by German philosophers like Kant and Hegel, and it dominated British philosophy in the early twentieth century. Immanuel Kant was especially influential, and he is still taught in most philosophy courses today. Kant thought that reality-in-itself is completely unknowable, but that human thought constructs reality-as-appearance (as we see it), and that human reason compels us to think of persons as free moral agents, not determined by the material world. Materialism, Kant thought, confuses appearance with reality. So even though we cannot know reality-in-itself, we must think of it as personal.

As I approach the topic of philosophical idealism, I will begin with some major philosophical questions raised by the natural sciences: does the objective world really consist only of the basic properties identified by physics? Is it governed by universal and unbreakable laws? Do those laws determine everything that happens, so that no alternatives are even possible?

Affirmative answers to these questions are very ambitious dogmas or postulates indeed; and they could not be confirmed by observation. We cannot observe the unobserved; we cannot be sure that laws of nature are never broken; and we can never know that nothing could have happened except what did happen. The postulates that physics can accurately and adequately describe what the unobserved world is like, that absolute laws of nature in some mysterious sense exist, and that there is one and only one possible effect of every cause, seem to be oddly arbitrary. Why should it be so?

Perhaps these are the basic postulates which helped modern science to get going. Only if we think that the human mind is capable of understanding the structure of nature, only if we think that there are mathematically describable laws or general principles of causality in nature, and only if we think that causality is universal, so that there is always a reason why anything happens, that nothing happens that cannot be accounted for by reference to some general rational principle, is modern science possible. These are, as Immanuel Kant put it, necessary conditions of the possibility of natural science (at least of a Newtonian sort).

But there is a paradox about these postulates. They give human thought and imagination a central role in comprehending the nature of reality. Human thinking, especially in inventing systems of mathematics and in devising cunning experiments to see how nature behaves, is assumed to be adequate for an understanding of nature.

But can we trust human reason? "Reason is the slave of the passions," said David Hume. How can we have the arrogance to think that the petty human mind – the product, according to some evolutionary views, of millions of random genetic copying-mistakes and accidents – is capable of understanding the origin of worlds or the ultimate nature of things? Perhaps, said Hume, we should accept that habit or custom controls human conduct. We just think the way our brains are set up to think, and they are set up that way, because brains with those thoughts in them have enabled organisms to survive and reproduce better than brains without such thoughts. Hume did not know about evolution. But he certainly would have approved of it, since he believed that enlightened Scottish intellectuals were more evolved than the common herd of humanity.

Brains that thought that you could never predict what was going to happen next died out, because they never learned from experience. Only brains that assumed the future would be like the past had the sense to flee from predators, and only those brains survived. Over many centuries a stock of common-sense beliefs builds up, simply because brains without those beliefs get wiped out. Such beliefs would include the belief that there are predators out there even when you don't observe them (the principle of objective existence), that predators are going to behave in regular and more or less predictable ways (the principle of induction), and that the same predator always produces the same effect – namely, once you are caught you will be eaten (the principle of efficient causality).

Of course this is just a way of saying that true beliefs tend to be more useful than false beliefs. The reason these sorts of beliefs have survival-value is that they are true; they say what reality is like. You could say that the beliefs are based on long and repeated observations by many people, some but not all of whom got eaten. They are not just abstract rational principles, thought up in some primeval cave.

I was once asked to contribute the section on philosophy in a Reader's Digest book, *The Last Two Million Years*. I agreed to write the first half and, before the commissioning editors had quite realized what was going on, collected quite a nice fee for saying, correctly, that as far as we know nothing happened in philosophy for the first million years. They nevertheless produced some pretty pictures from the Lascaux Caves, which perhaps could, by a large stretch of the imagination, be called philosophical (that is to say, nobody is quite sure what they are about). Regrettably I missed the opportunity to write a chapter on Neanderthal philosophy, which did not, as it turned out, have a very good survival-value.

Toward the unknown

Returning to the question of basic evolved beliefs, the point remains that these beliefs go well beyond simple observation. They begin from observations, but what they do is organize our sense-perceptions so that we interpret these perceptions as perceptions of entities which have objective existence, which threaten, entertain or eat us, and which behave in more or less predictable ways. Such organizing principles are not arbitrary, since they can help us to eat other things before they eat us – a skill at which humans are remarkably adept.

These principles no doubt form the basis of the more science-based principles of objectivity, causal law, and determinism. They are nonetheless very different. Common sense sees the world as consisting of predators and prey, not atoms and molecules. We see that predators behave in more or less regular ways, without thinking that they obey universal laws of nature. We think that we can sometimes escape the predator's leap, not that there is no alternative to being eaten. The idea of a Newtonian reality of deterministic and universal law is a leap of imagination that was first clearly formulated by Newton himself, even though it was presaged by some late medieval philosophers, as a combination of ideas of predestination and the creation of the universe by a rational all-determining being.

Moreover, the Newtonian picture omits entirely some other human basic evolved beliefs. Early humans developed a "theory of mind", that other animals have purposes and intentions partly hidden from us, but helping us to predict what they will do next. They developed a principle of reciprocity, that you can never quite be sure how other animals will react to you, but your attitude to them will be an important factor in how they subsequently behave. They developed a principle of responsibility, so that on many occasions you can choose between alternative actions, and you are responsible for that choice.

All these natural principles are hard to accommodate in a Newtonian scheme of nature. Minds, personal relationships, and free actions, are all alien to a wholly mechanistic view of objective reality. Yet it is precisely in scientific investigations that we must assume the importance of understanding and imagination, the cumulative cooperation of many meaningfully communicating minds, and the free selection of experimental conditions and mathematical axioms that will enable us to understand the physical world better.

Is it plausible to consider all this as a higher-order by-product of the unconscious, mechanically determined, exclusively rule-driven behaviour of huge numbers of fundamental particles, each of which is identical in nature to every other of the same sort? Locke baulked at the thought, as had Descartes before him. Thus they were driven to introduce minds into a Newtonian mechanistic scheme that left no room for them. Having constructed the machine of nature, they then had to introduce ghosts to pull the levers of the machine. But how insubstantial ghosts could pull solid material levers, or even where exactly the levers were to be found, remained a mystery.

Perhaps the solution is not to get rid of the ghosts, but to dismantle the machine and start again. That is precisely what happened in the early twentieth century with the advent of quantum mechanics. The machine itself began to disappear. Ryle and Wittgenstein had that thought, too. But they preferred to bypass the findings of the new physics, and to resort to the sort of common-sense beliefs that had preceded physics, and that left questions of the nature of reality as pseudo-problems that could be ignored.

Some physicists agree and regard philosophy as a waste of time. We can do the maths, make the predictions, construct the nano-devices. But we do not need to give any theoretical interpretation to what we are doing. Others, however, feel the need to relate our mathematical computations to our understanding of the world, and to answer the question of what the world is objectively like. But maybe what quantum physics suggests is that the question is unanswerable. For quantum physicists like Bernard d'Espagnat objective reality is forever "veiled" from human knowledge, and all we can know is how things appear to us when we observe them (when we collapse wave-functions) in laboratory conditions. Perhaps there is no way of knowing what reality is like in itself, apart from human observation of it. We know how the world appears to us, but its inner reality remains forever veiled. That possibility introduces my sixth philosophical theory about what the world is really like, the theory that human knowledge is confined to how the objective world appears to our minds and senses, but that the world in itself is wholly unknowable. Nevertheless, in some sense the world as we know it is a product of mind. In the history of philosophy, that is the view of Immanuel Kant, who called it "transcendental idealism", but in his later writings said that he preferred the phrase **critical idealism** (Theory 6).

Immanuel Kant and unknowable reality

Most classical philosophers have been idealists – they have thought that the ultimate character of reality is mind-like. But in modern philosophy the most influential name is that of Immanuel Kant. If we want to trace the roots of modern forms of idealism, we have to start with Kant. There is quite a lot of misunderstanding of his views – he is thought to have undermined the possibility of metaphysics and to have destroyed all arguments for God, for example. On the contrary, his aim was to place metaphysics on a firm footing, and to defend belief in God as rationally necessary (though not founded on theoretical arguments about causality).

Kant's views are very complex, but it is worth exploring them, as they provide the basis for taking modern idealism seriously. He held that space and time themselves, which seem so objective, are in fact forms of our intuition. That is, they are a framework the mind constructs to build a map in which our sense-perceptions can be located. The map is mind-constructed, and if we take away mind, we have no way of saying what is left. This may seem an extremely odd view, but it receives some corroboration from modern physics. In quantum physics our view of space as a three-dimensional Euclidean container, and of time as a kind of cosmic clock which ticks at an absolute rate, adding second to second as we pass through it, is a purely subjective condition of our perception, which does not copy what objectively exists. Quantum physicists tend to say that space-time is non-Euclidean, and is part of a multi-dimensional reality in which space and time may become, under certain conditions, interchangeable. Superstring field theorists say that space and time are perceptually selected fragments of a ten-dimensional hyperworld, and do not exist objectively as the Euclidean space and flowing time that we perceive them to be. Such things can be mathematically expressed, but if we try to imagine what such a strange world is like, imagination fails. Things in themselves are totally beyond our categories of thought.

It seems, then, that the whole of experienced space-time, and everything in it, is a construction of the mind, and would not exist without the mind. Some philosophers talk about "constructions of the brain" rather than constructions of the mind. But that is a fairly crude mistake, since the brain is a material thing in space-time, and therefore cannot be what constructs the reality of experienced space-time. The brain, like all material things, is a construct of the mind and would not exist as it appears to us without that constructive activity of the mind. So the world as we see it is not a construction of the brain, but the world as we see it (including the brain) is a construction of the mind.

That is enough to refute the simple materialist view that

nothing exists, or even can exist, outside of space and time. Beyond observed space-time, there are at least two things. One is the unknowable world of things in themselves and the other is the mind that constructs the world of appearances, by its creative interaction with things in themselves.

But if the mind is not an appearance (since it constructs the world of appearances), it must be a thing in itself. Or, to be more precise, what appears to us as the constructive activity of the mind in producing the world of appearances, is also an expression of an entity in the world of things in themselves.

Even if the mind as we experience its activity is an appearance, it is as real an appearance as the world of physical objects we sense. It is not the case, as Gilbert Ryle seems to say, that physical objects (bodies) are obviously real, whereas minds (creative intellectual acts that constitute the world of sense-perceptions and thoughts) are ghosts. On the contrary, both bodies and minds are appearances of an objective reality. They have an equally real (or unreal) status.

The personal world

Ryle would of course object that this is even worse than Cartesian dualism. His view is that in the Cartesian world we never know what is going on in other minds. Minds are locked in permanent isolation and never meet. But at least bodies meet. That is enough. We do not need these private islands where minds spend their lives in solitary confinement.

The Kantian world is much worse. Not only are minds in isolation. The whole of the experienced world is put into isolation, minds, bodies, and all. People cannot ever get out of their own private worlds or know what is going on in anybody else's world. Bodies never meet, for bodies are just parts of essentially private worlds. We are condemned forever to never meet anyone else, and never to know what is really going on. All of us are condemned to permanent ignorance and illusion, from which there is no escape. Is that better than Descartes?

Ryle is right. We cannot have a world in which knowledge depends upon making untestable inferences to hidden processes. But Kant does not think that we make inferences to the external existence of objects. Kant proposes that from the very first we interpret what we experience *as* experience *of* a world of objects. Our interpretations of the world are not just passive receptions of inert sensations. We are not faced with a lot of private sensations from which we subsequently have to infer the untestable assumption of an external world and other people. Experience is in a sense not shared with anyone else. But that is a realization that comes only from the much later sophisticated reflection that not everyone sees the world as I do.

From the very first, Kant argues, human thinking is an active power that necessarily interprets experience as experience of a world of continuing substances in causal interaction. That is, we interpret the coloured shapes we see *as* appearances of external objects which we encounter through these perceptions. This is a basic interpretative activity of the mind. We do not see sensations. We see objects, presented to us via sensations. Experience comes to us already interpreted by thought. We are aware both that something beyond our control is given to us in experience, and also that thinking actively interprets that "something" as a world of causally interacting substances. We are never isolated and alone. On the contrary, we are always encountering other objects and actively responding to them. We are active agents in a world of active agents. That is not an inference; it is a necessary condition of the possibility of knowledge, both in science and in everyday experience of personal relationships.

To know anything you need both perceptions – sensory data – and concepts – thoughts. So of the world beyond our perceptions, of reality in itself, there can be no theoretical knowledge. This is the proper reply, Kant thinks, both to common sense (naive) realists and to reductive materialists. They both think they know what there is, but both are mistaken. Kant does not know what there is (not theoretically, anyway). But, whatever it is, it must produce the appearances we see and the active minds that interpret them. There is a hidden reality, and the mind plays a positive creative role in interpreting its appearances. This provides the key to understanding what Kant always regarded as the most important, and most misunderstood, part of his philosophy: that which reason forbids me to know, reason compels me to believe.

The limits of reason

Kant argues that if reason claims to tell the truth about ultimate reality it leads to contradictions (he calls these "antimonies"). But we do know that if there are appearances, then there must be a reality that appears. In the world of appearances, we seek determining causes for everything. We actually insist that nature conforms to our demand for causes for all events. It is a condition of the possibility of scientific knowledge of the world that we think of the world as consisting of continuing substances in a succession of regular and predictable causal relationships. That is no mere whim, as if it were no better than being inclined to think of the world as moved about by the arbitrary acts of millions of fairies. These inclinations are rational, because they are the very conditions of the possibility of our understanding of an intelligible world. And they are confirmed by constant experience, as science continually finds out more about the natural world.

Just as reason (or understanding, in Kant's terminology) lays down the conditions of the possibility of scientific knowledge, so reason lays down the conditions of a complete rational explanation of the world, including the non-scientific facts of subjective consciousness, freedom, value, and purpose. These conditions cannot be completely confirmed by any specific experience, so they remain postulates – not irrational leaps of faith, but rational postulates that cannot be fully confirmed by experience.

The postulates of reason, according to Kant, have both a negative and a positive sense. In their negative sense, they show that materialism, naturalism, and fatalism are indefensible, according to

Kant's *Prolegomena to any Future Metaphysic*. Materialism is the view that the mind is nothing but a material thing, whereas Kant shows, he thinks, that it is the part-creator of reality-as-appearance. Naturalism is the view that nature is self-sufficient, whereas Kant shows that nature is the appearance of an underlying and unknowable reality. And fatalism is the view that all human acts are products of blind necessity, whereas Kant shows that they may indeed be free in reality, even though we can never prove that they are.

To many philosophers, it sounds impressive to say that the experienced world is only an appearance of a very different underlying reality. But it is not quite so impressive when it is added that we know nothing at all about such a reality. Kant's position of complete theoretical agnosticism about the world of things-in-themselves does not quite ring true.

The leap of reason

It is at this point that "faith" comes into the picture, and gives a positive sense to the postulates of reason. Faith, for Kant, has absolutely nothing to do with revelation or religious authority, both of which he hated so much that he never went to church and regarded kneeling down to pray as an affront to human dignity. Kant was a great defender of autonomy, of deciding things for yourself, and he tried to get all his disciples to take his word for it that they should decide things for themselves. He added of course that if they decided correctly, they would all agree with him, since he always made the most rational decisions. Insofar as they disagreed, they were not being fully rational.

Kantian faith is the positive acceptance of the unprovable but fully rational postulates of reason on practical or moral (not religious) grounds. Kant wrote three "critiques of reason", in which he set out to show the limits of reason and its positive role in human thought. At this point I am only concerned with the first two critiques. His first critique, the *Critique of Pure Reason*, was concerned with examining the role of theoretical reason in helping us to achieve knowledge in science. He argued that it is a condition of the possibility of doing science that you accept some necessary postulates of understanding (most importantly, the objective existence of substances and of causality).

His second critique, the *Critique of Practical Reason*, went on to discuss the role of reason in practical action and especially in morality. He argued that it is a condition of the possibility of morality that you accept some postulates of reason (most importantly, the objective existence of free agents who are able to act on rationally chosen principles). Having shown that science does not give a theoretical account of things-in-themselves, he now suggests that morality gives a special sort of insight into that veiled reality. At least it compels us to *think* of it in a particular way (as a world of free agents), even though we cannot theoretically establish our beliefs.

Reason thus plays a positive role in human knowledge. In theoretical matters it requires sense-experience to confirm its postulates. But humans not only think and understand. They also act and set and pursue goals that they believe to be good. Is this a function of reason also? Can reason set goals of action, and are we free to pursue them? For Kant, reason does set two general goals of action – the happiness of others and one's own perfection, "the fullest use of one's free powers".

But if reason sets such goals, then reason must be assumed to possess a causal role in the world, setting goals of action which I can then pursue. This entails two beliefs – that I am free to set and pursue rational goals and that it is possible to achieve them (otherwise it would not be a rational pursuit). Thereby results one of Kant's major conclusions: I can never theoretically prove the human will is free. But for rational action and moral commitment to be possible, I must presuppose freedom in practice. Whatever my theoretical indecisions, I must commit myself in practice, and I know that I should commit myself to the wholly good.

Moreover, if I really think free commitment to realizing goodness is reasonable, I must believe that the good – which consists of both happiness and that form of self-cultivation which is virtue – is achievable, even in a corrupted world. Kant's point is that if moral action is to be fully reasonable, and not just a matter of arbitrary decision, I must assume that what I am trying to achieve is possible. So fully rational moral action must commit itself to the hope that a world in which happiness is realized in accordance with the practice of virtue can and will exist. That is a presupposition of the rationality of the real world to which the human will commits itself in genuine moral action. For if reality is rationally structured, it will exist in order to realize an envisaged good, and the realization of that good is assured by the rational order of reality.

Kant is not, after all, a total agnostic. He believes there can be no knowledge or proof of the nature of the world beyond the senses. But he knows there is and must be such a world. The world of appearance is a world constituted by both an unknown objective reality and the constitutive activity of the mind, which in itself is also unknown.

But where theory may hesitate, persons must act. This is not as far from Hume as it may seem. Hume also is sceptical about transcendent metaphysical truths obtainable by reason. Hume also thinks we must act on the basis of our human sentiments and habitual inclinations to believe. But whereas Hume thinks that we are driven by passions and habits, which we cannot help, Kant insists that there are rational goals of action, that human persons are free, autonomous (capable of direction by their own free decisions), and that we must assume (without theoretical proof) whatever is necessary to embrace that freedom.

In this way Kant qualifies his view that we can know nothing of reality in itself. Though that is true of theoretical or testable knowledge, in moral action we commit ourselves to thinking of objective reality in a specific way, as a realm of autonomous rational agents. The limitation of theoretical knowledge to appearances means that such a commitment cannot either be established or disproved theoretically. In that situation, practice takes priority over theory, and, as Kierkegaard was later to put it, we may passionately commit ourselves to what is theoretically uncertain. For Kant, such passionate commitment is not irrational or non-rational. It is supremely rational and a condition of accepting the reasonableness of human moral freedom. It is a leap of reason, not a leap of faith.

Chapter Four

Putting minds first

Kant's denial of all theoretical knowledge of reality was judged by many philosophers who followed him to be implausible. Other forms of idealism, the best known of which is that of Hegel, more boldly affirm that we can know something about reality-in-itself, namely, that it really is mind-like. There are other forms of idealism too. Many of them can be found in Indian philosophy. In the West, one of them is process philosophy, formulated by the British philosopher and mathematician A. N. Whitehead, which claims that there are many mental realities, rather than just one dominating Absolute Mind. In all its forms, however, idealism is obviously opposed to materialism, and gives mind or consciousness a primary place in our idea of reality.

Kant says that the conceptual categories we use only have theoretical meaning within the realm of sense-experience. Yet he also holds that there is a reality beyond sense-experience, of which the sensory world is an appearance. But how can he even say that there is a realm beyond sense-experience, which is the hidden cause of our sense-experiences? He is using the categories of substance (things-in-themselves are described as things, after all), existence, and causality, which should have no meaning. He is even describing the things-in-themselves as noumenal (which means "mind-like" or "only apprehensible by mind"), intelligible or conceptual as opposed to sensory.

Although the freedom of the self cannot be proved by induction or by empirical methods, it must, he says, be postulated as a condition of moral action. The ideas of reason do not have theoretical meaning, but we must act *as if* they are true of the noumenal world, and the justification for this is that they must be used to achieve unity in our knowledge and to underpin moral action. It is far from satisfactory, however, to hold that we must act as if something is true, when we know it is not, and when we have no idea, theoretically speaking, of what is true. To hold that this is a totally rational procedure stretches the meaning of rationality beyond any reasonable limits.

The trouble is that Kant provides a wholly mechanistic and deterministic view of phenomena, while free action and the judgments of understanding and reason are allocated to a non-mechanistic and non-deterministic (but also non-temporal and non-spatial) realm. This means that I must regard my moral actions as free and undetermined – but only in a noumenal realm beyond space and time.

For most of us, however, free acts take place in time. I am free when I perform a specific action. It is not really much help to say that all my specific actions in time are determined, but that there is some sort of non-temporal freedom as well. The attempt to make sense of this even leads Kant at one point to say that perhaps the place where I am born is freely chosen by me in a non-temporal sense, and that is dangerously near to saying that I am poor and oppressed because I choose to be. I do not think we want to go there. This is worse than a ghost in a machine; it is something completely invisible inside the appearance of a machine. And that threatens to undermine the very morality and rationality the Kantian system was designed to protect.

The personal, the moral, and the scientific have to be integrated in a better way than this. It is actually Kant and not Descartes who is the chief proponent of the myth against which Ryle inveighs. Descartes doubted only for a while, and in a purely hypothetical way. But Kant advocates an utter scepticism about what reality-in-itself is like. His doubt is total and irrevocable. Of course Kant protests that his philosophy leaves everything as it is, in this phenomenal world. That is why he protests (too much?) that he is not an "idealist", in the sense of being a person who thinks physical objects are only ideas in the mind or that the whole of reality is in the mind of a perceiver.

But the fact is that Kant does think that the whole of reality *as it is perceived* is a product of the mind of the perceiver. The term he preferred for this philosophical outlook was "critical idealism". There is an unknowable reality underlying the world of appearances, but it adds nothing at all to theoretical knowledge. It could simply be ignored, except that it gives the mind a constitutive and active and essential role in experience. Thus it leads us to think of reality-in-itself as mind-like, even though we have no theoretical knowledge of it. Reason does in fact have something to say about the world of things-in-themselves. But it says it only from a practical (Kant says, a "regulative") point of view, for the sake of grounding and motivating our moral action and our sense of the intrinsic moral worth of human persons.

Many modern philosophers would recommend avoiding this conclusion by getting rid of things-in-themselves, and reverting to some sort of realism. I think Ryle did that. The trouble is that once you recognize the dependence of human knowledge of the world upon the specific structure of human senses and brains, and once you give thought a constructive part in building up human knowledge, you do seem to be stuck with the conclusion that the world we perceive is largely a product of our perceptual and conceptual apparatus. Even our brains are parts of the perceived world of appearances. Kant is not saying that you only have the appearance of a brain. His assertion is that your brain is only an appearance – so it cannot be what constructs the world of appearances.

Still, Kant could not get rid of the suspicion that there must be some reality underlying the appearances. Neither could many philosophers after Kant, the best known of whom is probably Hegel, who said that if you can posit that there are things-in-themselves, you must also posit that the mind has some access to what those things really are. Kant really believed this anyway, deep down, but his philosophical system forced him to say that we could have no theoretical knowledge of reality-in-itself. We are moving toward a more fully-fledged statement of philosophical idealism.

The priority of mind

In order to get to a more robust form of idealism, we only have to discard the idea, central to Kant's theoretical philosophy, that concepts without "intuitions" or perceptions are empty. There are some concepts (roughly, the ones Kant called "ideas") that are not conclusively confirmable by sense-observation, but that may be basic to our metaphysical scheme. These will include concepts suggested by reflection upon the causal activity of the mind in both theoretical knowledge and moral action.

Kant is convinced that his critical philosophy shows materialism to be false. Minds, since they play a constructive part in creating the objects of knowledge, cannot be just objects of empirical knowledge (brains). Minds are active in two main ways, theoretically and practically. Theoretically they interpret sense-experience in terms of a world of enduring objects having causal relations and often forming integrated wholes. They "see" the immediate and transitory data of the senses as mediating a reality beyond themselves. Thus they see the present as mediating the past, in remembering past data and identifying present data as integral parts of what has gone before. This is perhaps clearest in music, where we hear notes as parts of a tune, not as isolated sounds.

Minds also see the present as mediating the future, seeing possibilities for action over stretches of time. Minds see the present as mediating objectivity, a world of objects continuing to exist unobserved. Minds also see the present as mediating a sense of self, a continuing agent which integrates experiences into one unique totality of "my experience". And minds see the present as often mediating other agent selves, with goals that may block or help their own.

In all these ways, I have the idea of myself as a continuing cognitive agent among others in a common world – something that perception without thought could not generate. My inner mental life of perceptions and thoughts does not, as Ryle suggests, lock me into a private world that could never encounter or be known by others. On the contrary, it is because minds have private thoughts and experiences that they are of interest to others, and that they always remain to some extent mysterious and intriguing. But it is because minds interpret their sense-perceptions as mediating a world of objects and persons (intentional agents) that they know there are others to find intriguing. Persons meet through the mutual interpretative mediation of their thoughts, through language, by which marks or sounds are taken as mediating meaning beyond their sensory appearances.

Minds are also active practically. They consider future possibilities and evaluate them. They choose courses of action and initiate them. They make moral decisions and to some extent shape their own characters by the habitual patterns of action that they choose over time. So persons are praised or blamed for their actions, assuming that they could have chosen otherwise, and that they knew the moral quality of what they were doing.

We may not know what the veiled reality underlying physical objects is. But there is a good case for saying that we do know what the reality underlying our own mental activity is. That reality is known, not through perception, but in the cognitive and moral activity of the self. At this point reality is known in and through its activity, and that activity is the activity of mind, of free and conscious interpretation and choice.

Kant said that we do not know what the mind is in itself; we only know its phenomenal acts. But the mind is known in itself precisely in its activity. Mental activity is not something that appears to us in one way, but exists in itself in another way. Mind is known in its actions, which are not appearances of objects – that was Hume's mistake when he tried to find the self as an object. The self is not an object that can be perceived like a block of wood or a tree. The self is the unobservable agent that makes all experience of the sensory world possible and is the source of all responsible actions in that world.

It is thus the activity of the self that gives access to reality, and which creates for us the world of appearances. The primary sense of reality-in-itself that we have is that it has the character of mind, of active mediating knowledge, and responsible choice. To make such a blunt assertion as this is to move beyond Kant's agnosticism to a more fully-fledged idealism, affirming that we are capable of knowing that the basic character of reality is mind or consciousness.

Absolute idealism

Idealists are aware that there are many human (and perhaps other finite) minds. They claim that the material world (which is the phenomenal world, the world as we know it through perception) exists as an environment created by a primordial mind in which finite minds can exist in mutual self-expression and interaction.

This is about as far from materialism and as far from common-sense realism as it is possible to get. It totally reverses the modern myth that minds are by-products of a purely material evolutionary process, completely determined by physical events in their bodies and brains. What it says is that physical events as we perceive and know them are appearances constructed by minds. What the reality underlying those appearances may be in detail we do not know.

But since minds are the only sorts of reality we know to belong to the world of things-in-themselves, it is reasonable to think that reality does not exist without mind and consciousness, evaluation and intention, understanding and action. Minds are irreducible elements of reality and they play a constructive role in the existence of the phenomenal world that we perceive and know. Minds are not illusory ghosts in real machines. On the contrary, machines are spectral, transitory phenomena appearing to an intelligible world of minds.

What idealists maintain is that the ultimate nature of reality itself is mind-like, and that human and other finite minds are the best clues we have to what objective reality is like. The cosmos is not a mindless, unconscious, valueless, purposeless, yet somehow strangely intelligible, mechanism. Such a view is the result of extrapolating a machine-model, very useful in many scientific contexts, to provide the most comprehensive and adequate picture of the real cosmos.

Idealists propose that the human mind provides a better model from which to extrapolate to the cosmos as a whole. That is not because the cosmos looks like a very large human person or because there is some large person hovering just beyond the cosmos. It is because human minds play a creative and constructive role in producing the phenomenal world. They seem to point to a level of reality that is not merely phenomenal or an appearance to consciousness. Human minds generate an idea of reality as mind-like in a way that far transcends human mentality, yet that does include something like consciousness, value, and purpose as essential parts of its nature.

There are many forms of idealism. Kant's critical idealism is just a little too agnostic for most idealists. Some philosophers, like McTaggart, have proposed that a society of minds underlies and gives rise to our physical cosmos. Perhaps the best-known European idealist, Hegel, hypothesized that there is just one Absolute Mind or Spirit which progressively realizes its nature in the history of the cosmos. This form of idealism, often called **absolute idealism**

(Theory 7), is what I am calling the seventh philosophical view. It is found as a major strand in the Indian philosophical traditions, too. Sankara, an eighth-century sage and saint, founded the school of *Advaita* – non-dualism – which holds that the whole of the cosmos and everything in it is an appearance of one Supreme Spirit. Though that Spirit – *Brahman* – is unknowable in its inner nature, it makes itself known as *sat-cit-ananda,* an infinite reality of intelligence and bliss. Finite minds are appearances of that one Absolute, and each human person can come to know itself as a part of that Absolute Mind, not a separate entity.

There is an interpretation of absolute idealism to which I should like to draw attention, because it gives a much more positive role to the material world than the rather negative assertion of *Advaita* that matter and individual minds are in the end illusions. It is best approached through the work of another Indian philosopher, Ramanuja, probably a twelfth-century thinker, who founded the philosophical school of *Vishist-advaita* **Vedanta** or qualified non-dualism. This school is non-dualist, because it stresses that all things and all persons are parts or expressions of one supreme reality of Spirit. But it places strong emphasis on personal autonomy and relationship. So Spirit realizes itself by "becoming many", by relating to partly autonomous finite spirits which together express the nature of Mind. On this interpretation, it is perhaps clearer that the cosmos of finite persons is not just some sort of illusion, which should ideally be transcended. The cosmos is more like the positive "play" (*lila*) of Spirit, with a positive function of allowing relational properties like cooperation and friendship to exist as proper parts of the self-expression of Absolute Spirit. The ideal is a sort of diversity-in-unity, in which differences remain, but are united in a wider whole. I think that this is rather close to what Hegel meant to convey, though Hegel seemed to suffer from a congenital inability to convey anything very clearly.

Process philosophy

A rather different form of idealism is more radically pluralistic, and gives causal priority not to one Absolute Spirit, but to a huge, possibly infinite, number of entities, which make up the physical universe. Each of these entities has a psychic or mental aspect, as well as an outer or physical aspect. Bertrand Russell believed such a view for at least two days, calling it "neutral **monism**". I prefer to call it **pluralistic idealism** (Theory 8), because it gives causal priority to the inner or mind-like aspects of events.

This may seem very unrealistic if it entails that even rocks and trees are conscious and have feelings, feeling hurt when they get moved around or chopped down. We may, however, confine consciousness as we experience it to higher organisms with brains, and yet say that all physical entities also have an "inner" nature that is a sort of embryonic consciousness, an unseen centre of capacities and powers that forms the heart of their being. Such a view – the eighth and mercifully, you may think, the last view that I will consider – has received an extensive exposition in A. N. Whitehead's "Process and Reality" – a series of Gifford lectures that is immensely complex and difficult in detail, but contains some basically simple ideas that reframe traditional metaphysical views in the light of modern science.

One of these simple ideas is that all events have an inner nature, hidden from external observation, which is the source of the creativity that drives the cosmos onwards in time. This philosophy, influenced in part by new developments in mathematical physics, can fairly be seen as a form of radically pluralistic idealism.

Like most really original philosophers, Whitehead begins his philosophy by denying what most other philosophers take to be absolutely certain. Kant, for example, held that we necessarily interpret the world as a collection of substances which continue to exist even when all their non-essential properties change. Whitehead, however, denied that there are any substances at all. There are only processes, chains of events, not held together by any underlying substance. Whitehead's view is that events are discrete existents, and that the chains they form are complexes in which the individual creativity of huge, perhaps infinite, numbers of basic events is the true cause of change in the phenomenal world.

Whitehead, like many philosophers, devises a technical vocabulary that is at times almost impenetrable. But with a bit of over-simplification, his basic scheme is this: the world is made up of huge numbers of "actual occasions" or events, which are tiny blobs of "feeling". Each one lasts only for a split second, coming into being and perishing in the blink of an eye. Each one "prehends" or internally registers influences from a set of other events immediately preceding it. And each one then creatively projects into the future a new integration of these prehensions, which is passed on to its immediately succeeding actual occasions. These occasions form the process of actual being. Even though they "feel", they are not conscious, so feeling is a word for their internal structure, not for their emotional state.

Actual occasions form complex unities, in which a dominant event presides over a large array of smaller events in an organic whole. The human sense of self is a product of a vast array of actual occasions, organized into a complex organic unity, the human body, under the partial control of a dominant actual occasion which is fully conscious. Yet this dominant occasion, like all others, is in fact a series of evanescent events succeeding each other in a continuous sequence, maintaining the process of prehension and creativity that constitutes our actual world.

To many people this will seem a strange scheme, and it need not be taken too strictly. As with many philosophical systems, it may be wise to accept some general insights while resisting the intricacies of detail that seem to go with devising a grand philosophical system. Whitehead himself is alleged to have said, as he was dying, "I want no disciples" – to which of course those around him said, "Yes, Master." Process thought is not a final dogmatic system. It is more a spur to thinking in new ways about our complex universe.

We might pick out its main elements as being these: the world consists of a constant flow of transient moments, a "process". There is not a sharp dualistic disjunction between mind and matter. Matter is formed of "low-grade" events, and mind of "high-grade" events, but there is a continuity of being and a development of new characteristics as organic forms get more complex. What drives the process is not a set of mechanical and blind repetitive routines, but continual creativity and novelty, aiming overall at greater harmony and beauty and some sort of realization of the possibilities inherent in each new situation – but also realizing many conflicting and negative (narrowly self-satisfying) possibilities as an inevitable corollary of the system.

Absolute idealists would give a more positive causal role to Absolute Spirit, and might also feel that there is an important distinction of kind between conscious selves that can know and respond responsibly to their situation and the "lower-grade" events that have no consciousness, knowledge or freedom of action. Yet Whitehead's form of pluralistic idealism presents a philosophical hypothesis that takes account of the continuity and emergent development of the natural world and stresses the value of creativity, individuality, and freedom in nature that can be overlooked in some forms of absolute idealism.

Both forms of idealism, absolute and pluralistic, if taken to extremes, may put the concept of persons as autonomous, free, rational agents in question. The seventh theory, the idea that persons are all parts of one cosmic mind, may subordinate individuals completely to one all-determining reality, so that the cosmos becomes nothing but the progressive realization of "Absolute Spirit". Hegel has, probably unfairly, often been accused of this.

The eighth theory, that persons are chains of actual occasions, may undermine the idea of persons as continuing intelligent substances, seeing them as transitory parts of a much wider complex flow of events. Thus a major problem for idealism is to formulate an adequate concept of human personhood.

Ryle does not explicitly deal with the question of what constitutes a human person. I suspect he would say that the way we use language shows that we all know what a person is – not a rock, not an animal, and not an angel. I am not so sanguine. I think there is no more important question in the whole of philosophy and in the whole of life than that of what a person really is. Is a person a by-product of purposeless and blind physical forces, as materialists suppose? Or a single continuous autonomous rational agent, as Descartes thought? A particular finite expression of one universal mind, as Hegel claimed? Or part of an endless stream of sensations, thoughts, and feelings, of actual occasions, as Whitehead asserted?

To answer these questions, we have to have some theory about what is really real, since persons are certainly parts of reality. That is why I have set out eight main theories of the "really real": phenomenalism, common-sense or naive realism, materialism, dualism, epiphenomenalism, critical idealism, absolute idealism, and pluralistic idealism.

I have argued that there are good reasons for rejecting phenomenalism, naive realism, and materialism, and I do not much care for epiphenomenalism and critical idealism. But I have yet to deal with Ryle's objections to **Cartesian dualism**, which I need to do because I am aiming to develop a view of human persons that lies somewhere between Descartes, as traditionally understood, and a form of idealism.

I believe that persons are continuing centres of consciousness and responsible moral agency. I have said that a process view of persons may threaten to undermine this position. However, I actually think that process thought need not conflict with a view of persons as autonomous continuing selves – in Descartes' terms, as "thinking substances". In the next chapter I will try to show that this is so.

Chapter Five

Questions of personal identity

What is the nature of human persons? Are they aspects of one Absolute Mind (as in Hegel) or complex combinations of a huge number of mind-like events (as in Whitehead) or something else? I argue that human persons are primarily chains of experiences — thoughts, perceptions, feelings, and sensations — and actions (as in Process and some Buddhist forms of pluralistic idealism). But these chains are "owned" by continuing subjects ("mental substances") who give them their unique identity. It is thus possible to speak, as Descartes did, of continuing mental substances, and to emphasize that those substances ("minds" or "souls") are primarily made up of inner experiences and intentions.

So far I have tried to show that there are good philosophical arguments for idealism, and I have hinted that I intend to defend some form of Cartesian dualism, though not the most radical form (which I think is often wrongly ascribed to Descartes). The Cartesian view maintains that human persons are continuing mental substances, "thinking things". Idealist views may hold that persons are aspects of one Absolute Mind or that they are composed of streams of "actual occasions", as in Whitehead. In defending a form of Cartesian dualism, I want to suggest that there are varieties of idealism that can accommodate that form of dualism, and that such a combination of views may provide the most adequate account of what human persons are.

I will begin the discussion with a consideration of pluralistic idealism, because I think it is a good starting point for seeing what might be meant by considering persons as continuing substances. One reason for thinking of persons as substances has been that this idea enables us to think of a person as "the same" person through many changes of personality or in physical and mental properties. But is the idea of "substance" really helpful here, and what role does it play? Reflection on a view like process philosophy that explicitly denies the idea of "substance" might help to clarify the issue.

According to process philosophy, there are no continuing substances, whose properties may change while the underlying substance remains the same. There is just a continual flow of properties, some of which we group together when we speak of things continuing to exist as "the same things". Instead of saying, "The tree (a substance) has green leaves (properties), but they will turn red and fall off in winter (the properties change while the tree remains the same)," we should say, "This collection of leaf-like, branch-like, and trunk-like properties will remain the same in some respects, but it will change in others." Whether we call it "the same tree" or not is a matter of convention. We could say that it is not the same tree, because some of its properties are different. But we normally say that it is the same tree, because its trunk and branches are similar, and the leaves have changed in a generally regular and predictable way.

Some people think that an object can be called "the same" only if it is a continuous physical entity in space and time. A tree is the same tree only if it continues to occupy the same space (or a continuously connected series of spaces) throughout one uninterrupted time. But what if one day the tree disappeared and an exactly similar tree instantaneously appeared three feet to the right? Would it be the same tree? I guess that if trees consistently jumped three feet to the right on Tuesdays, we would get into the habit of calling them the same trees.

Would we say the same sort of thing about persons? What if my wife kept disappearing, but then reappeared after a short interval, three feet to the right? I guess I would get used to it in time. I would not say that I had lots of different wives in quick succession, all of them just like the last one. This seems to show that what matters is the process, the way in which properties succeed one another, and we do not need any invisible literally continuing substance to hold the properties together. My wife, and what I value about my wife, is not an invisible unchanging substance. It is the constantly changing, often surprising, always inventive yet reliable and dependable, chain of memories, feelings, likes and dislikes, habits, and goals, that I have lived with for forty-odd years. So far, the process view seems right.

However, lots of funny things can happen to processes. In Kafka's novel, *The Metamorphosis*, a man goes to bed one night and when he wakes up the next morning, he has changed into a large beetle. Whitehead would just say that lots of properties have changed, though what the man's wife would say is another question altogether. She would probably say that her husband was not as reliable as she had thought.

It is important for finding our way round in the world that people (collections of people-properties) do not suddenly change into collections of beetle-properties. We like to have regularities of change. Without them we could not do science, and it is doubtful whether we could have any long-term human relationships. Could you, for example, marry a man who might change into a beetle? Would you have to say, "Well, I married him for better or for worse. It just looks like things have suddenly got much worse"? Or should you have a new marriage vow: "I marry you for better or worse, unless you turn into a beetle (or some other large and offensive object)"? We like our processes to be fairly regular and predictable. Fortunately, they usually are.

So we might be tempted to say that persons are not permanent unchanging substances. They are complex chains of memories, perceptions, imaginings, evaluations, feelings, choices, and thoughts. They are processes. Buddhists manage to live with that thought without much trouble. Nevertheless, Buddhists notwithstanding, these processes are very special. They form unique kinds of unities, and in two main ways. It may turn out that these unities are an important part of what Descartes had in mind when he talked about "mental substances".

First, there is the unity of many memories, thoughts, perceptions, and feelings in one experience, a unity of experience. All the memories I have are my memories. Even if by mistake I have someone else's memories, when I have them they enter into one present consciousness which includes many thoughts and feelings and perceptions which are all mine. There is a unity of co-presence in consciousness.

Second, each chain of thoughts and perceptions is separated from every other chain in such a way that it is not possible for anyone to get from one chain to another. Your experiences remain yours and my experiences remain mine, and, it seems, never the twain shall meet. There is a unity of succession in consciousness.

Moreover, conscious events are not just passive experiences. They include active events like attending to or focussing on specific experiences, choosing to seek or avoid specific experiences, and forming intentions to bring future events about. If Kant is anywhere near right, the whole of conscious experience is the result of active acts of attention and interpretation, as well as of passive reception of data.

Given these facts, we can say that **one and the same person continues to exist if there is a unitary consciousness of co-present elements that flows smoothly and continuously through time without gaps, in ways that have at least partly been consciously and intentionally envisaged, evaluated,**

and chosen. That will do for a first shot at saying what a person is, and what it is for a person to continue as the same person over time and through change. It will need a little amendment to take account of some "gaps" in consciousness that obviously exist – when we go to sleep, for example – and that will come later in this chapter.

Technically, for process philosophers, each moment of choice could be seen as a new act, performed by a new, never-before-existing agent. But such choices are made in view of all the knowledge and memories in one consciousness at that time, and as part of a future-directed process whose constituent events are parts of one unique chain of such unitary conscious complexes. Assuming that there are no breakdowns or delusions in such knowledge and memory, and that the pursuit of longer-term goals proceeds by a series of overlapping intermediate steps, we call the series of events that forms one discrete "chain of events" or process the acts and states of one and the same person.

There is in fact no discernible difference between there being a succession of agent-causes, linked together by being members of one unique chain of unitary conscious states, and there being one agent that continues as the "same" throughout the existence of such a chain. As long as each agent remembers one and only one immediately past consciousness and intends to modify one and only one immediately future consciousness, this is just what it means to say that the same agent continues through that chain of experiences. So it turns out that a process view of persons as successions of acts and experiences of a unique kind does not differ, when properly examined, from a Cartesian view that there is one continuing mental substance that thinks, feels, imagines, and perceives.

You cannot peel the substance off from its thinkings and feelings as though it could continue intact without them. That which thinks and feels *is* the succession of active causes that are normally linked by a continuous chain of conscious events in a way that no other causes are. As David Hume said, I cannot "see" a causal agent in addition to all the causal agencies of attending, choosing, and intending, that are the contents of my consciousness. But I do not need to do so, since I am the collection of all my responsible actions – a collection that is still being formed – and there is nothing else that I need or should want to be.

Of course the normal process that leads us to speak of personal identity can go wrong. Bodies can radically change, by serious accidents or diseases, for example. The unity of co-presence in consciousness can fragment, as with so-called multiple personality, when different consciousnesses seem to connect with the same body. Memories and thoughts can become imagined or illogical, as when I seem to remember doing things I never did – which seems increasingly to happen as I get older. Actions can become wrongly directed toward their goals, or those goals may change and disappear from consciousness, so that I may obsessively perform actions over and over again, without any idea why.

Personal identity is a fragile process and often a matter of degree. There are no hard-edged boundaries that delineate when a person who has changed radically in some ways is or is not "the same person". The sort of body we have, the memories that haunt or delight us, the personality that disposes us to be good-humoured or acerbic, our basic evaluations and goals, are all important to being a human person. A major change in any of these aspects might make us wonder if we are the same person. A major change in most of them would probably incline us to say we are not. Nevertheless, there are some clear central, and it is to be hoped normal, cases where "being the same person" is not in doubt. We do not have to say that there is some invisible and undetectable substance that continues underneath all the changing states and properties. But in central cases, consciousness and responsible choice are important factors in determining identity of personhood. Mental factors, in other words, are crucially important in determining what persons are, in a way that material, bodily, factors are not, even if we do not want to be forced into the position of denying that humans who lack those factors are persons. Perhaps that may seem obvious. I hope it does. Yet it is something that tough-minded, eliminative materialists deny.

Memories and persons

So far we have a rough idea of how persons can continue to exist at different times and places. Philosophers, however, will not be satisfied with such a rough idea. They will try to test it to destruction in order to undermine the claim that persons are constituted by chains of memories, thoughts, and feelings. They do this by imagining how they can mix such chains of conscious experiences up in various ways, until we no longer know whether we are talking about the same person or not. If we can do that, they say, this attempt to say that persons are primarily defined by their conscious mental lives will have collapsed.

What would happen, for instance, if you took the memories of one person and put them into the mind of another person (perhaps by means of a brain transplant)? This may not seem impossible. It is quite possible that I may remember doing things that somebody else did (I may clearly remember winning Wimbledon, though Pete Sampras did so). The line between imagination, fantasy, and memory is very thin.

If I remember doing something I never did, have I become the person who did them (John Locke is often accused of thinking this)? Or if I remember doing something nobody ever did, have I become nobody?

The film *Total Recall*, starring Arnold Schwarzenegger and based on a story by Philip K. Dick, starts with the idea that future travel shops can save on their carbon footprint by not actually sending you anywhere. Instead, they implant memories that you have already been there in your brain. You pay for the memory of a holiday and, since you usually only remember the good bits, that is in many ways preferable to the hassle of actually travelling and possibly being disappointed.

The point of the film is that the hero changes his mind and escapes from the memory-implant machine. He then undergoes a series of increasingly alarming experiences, ending in him saving the planet from destruction. But this is exactly the adventure he had in fact paid for in the first place. So did he really escape or did he just falsely remember that he had escaped? We never find out. It's a pretty good story, even though my wife thinks I liked it because of the extreme violence in it. However, I know that it was the philosophical puzzles I liked (at least I think I know that, but I can't quite remember).

Suppose I remember killing someone, though I actually never did so (though no one knows that). I might confess to murder and sincerely regret what I think I did. Should I be punished for it? In the state of California, a philosophically minded defence lawyer has argued that his client, who actually did murder somebody, should not be punished, because he was not a continuing self, and the agent who committed the murder had ceased to exist long ago. Since then, he had been replaced many times by a number of other agents, and the present agent standing in court had only just begun to exist. So he could not have murdered anyone. The defence did not succeed. But why not?

It is not in question that we often have false memories and that we lose many memories. Do we have to remember something accurately before we can be punished or rewarded for it? Or could we receive a Nobel prize for a discovery we cannot remember making and that perhaps we have forgotten all about? The Oxford philosopher Derek Parfit imagines replacing half of his brain with half the brain of Greta Garbo. Would he then receive half of a lifetime achievement award for what she did? Or would it be he, or half of him, who had done it? Or would she never receive the award, because she had turned into someone else, namely Greta Parfit or possibly Derek Garbo?

The mind boggles. Normally, if I work hard for a long time I may deserve a reward, and if I have done many things that are harmful to others, I may deserve some sort of penalty. We do think about the future, and about the consequences of our actions. And we think about *our* future, not just somebody's future. If I save hard for my retirement, I will not be happy if somebody else gets my pension. The point is: I do not do things that will cause some good states later, whoever experiences those states. I do things, at least when I am being prudent rather than altruistic, that will cause good for an agent who is continuous with me now. The experience in future will include memories of me now and will be able to connect a whole series of actions with one continuing set of overlapping experiences.

In fact, no one could ever perform an action for their own future well-being if they did not believe they would exist in the future. But when we analyse it, what distinguishes me in the future is that there is a temporal continuity between successive sets of private experiences, to which no one else has direct access. "I" am constituted by a present unique set of experiences and actions, which continues into the future. So I realize that what happens to this present member of the chain of experiences is a consequence of what some past members of the chain have done. Conversely, what I do now will have consequences for some future agent/experient who is uniquely connected in time to this chain.

Most of the curious cases that philosophers have thought up are cases in which there is some pathological malfunction in the chain. It is imagined that some members of one mental chain are spliced into another mental chain. Those members will not have been caused by previous free and responsible acts in this chain, but they may have been caused by prior free acts in another chain from which they came.

The full story must of course include the fact that the chains have been tampered with, and that most instances of tampering will be criminal acts of psychological damage. A normally healthy person will remember events in his mental sequence and will be able to formulate long-term plans for future events in the sequence and act to realize them. Amnesia is an illness, which should be treated if possible, and which should not affect the treatment of present persons as (to the appropriate extent) a product of their previous free acts. Having false memories is also an illness, and since they do not represent genuine past causes, they have no implications for the present treatment of persons.

If, by some mischance, you have someone else's memories,

these should usually be treated as false memories. But if you can imagine two memory-chains being forcibly merged, like Parfit and Garbo, you would have one person with two distinct parallel sets of memories. If, unlike Parfit and Garbo, one was a serial killer and the other a saint, we would have a problem. Maybe we should think that both past persons have died, and we should just start again. We can only hope such a situation would never arise, since it would amount to penalizing the saint's past acts and overlooking those of the serial killer. But who said human life was perfectly fair anyway? We just have to muddle through doing the best we can. Human justice may work in normal cases, but break down in borderline, extremely improbable, situations.

My conclusion is that fantastic scenarios of memory-change do not undermine the claim that persons are largely constituted by continuous chains of memories, thoughts, and feelings, and that these are much more important than considerations of bodily continuity. This is what underlies our normal notions of moral responsibility, and the idea that we can develop our characters by attention and effort (or of course destroy them by distraction and indolence). It underpins our normal belief that human persons have a distinctive, perhaps unique, moral dignity and value.

Persons and bodies

I have stressed the importance of temporal continuity of experiences to our normal idea of continuing personhood. We also think that spatial continuity is important – there is normally a continuous spatial track between my body now and my body as it used to be, even though those bodies may look and feel very different. I have suggested, however, that strict spatial continuity may not be essential to my continuing to be the same person throughout a stretch of time. My body may disappear for periods of time, or it may move three feet to the right instantaneously, and I would still be the same person, as long as there is not more than one body that claims to be me.

Could we also dispense with strict temporal continuity? Could there be temporal gaps, so that I could altogether cease to exist for half an hour and then come back into existence again as the same person? In a sense, this already happens, because when I go to sleep there is a gap in the stream of conscious experiences, but that does not usually lead me to say that I die every night and somebody else wakes up in the morning. Of course my body has been there during the night. But I do not have to check that I have the same body before I can be sure exactly who I am when I wake up. I do not feel the need to employ people to keep watching me all night in case my body disappears. As far as I am concerned, my body might have disappeared during the night, and I would never notice. So my sense of being the same person cannot depend just on my having the same body all through the night (or a continuous series of closely connected bodies either). So it seems I can live with temporal gaps.

If that could happen for an hour or a night, what about a year? Or a million years? Just to make it worse, could I cease to exist for a million years, and reappear as the same person in quite a different body? Or would that be pushing the notion of personal identity too far?

Before we dismiss such an idea on the grounds that it is not normal, we need to remember that there is a very widespread human belief in reincarnation. Reincarnation offers a solution to the Parfit–Garbo problem. In some other life the merged persons, Parfit and Garbo, would demerge again, and both would get their due deserts in different bodies. But does it make sense to say that the same person might live again in a different body? Is reincarnation possible?

The philosopher Bernard Williams has argued that reincarnation is not even logically possible. Neither is the rather similar idea of resurrection – the idea that we might be resurrected, perhaps in a rather different or at least (we hope) reconstructed and improved body, after a huge temporal gap. It would need a very strong argument to show that reincarnation or resurrection could not possibly occur. But Williams does bring out some problems with the idea.

For instance, there are at this moment about three hundred people who claim that they used to be Napoleon Bonaparte. When, if ever, would we believe them? One vaguely alarming possibility is that they could all be Napoleon. The General has split into three hundred copies, rather like a human stem cell dividing into thousands of copies.

Some quantum physicists believe this actually happens, since every time one possible future is realized in one universe, an alternative possible future is realized in another universe. So Napoleon divided every time he did anything, and there are now millions of Napoleons in existence. But at least they are in different universes, and in any case they are all now dead (unless in some far away universe one Napoleon discovered the secret of eternal life).

Bernard Williams argued that none of these would be Napoleon, because you cannot have two identical things existing at the same time. Yet all these people would claim to be identical with the original Napoleon, and therefore they would all be identical with each other.

But what if one of them was the real Napoleon and all the others were fakes? That, says Williams, is impossible. Because of the lack of bodily continuity, they must all be fakes. And, he says, following this up with remorseless logic, if they are all fakes, then anyone who claims to be Napoleon but exists at a different time from Napoleon must be a fake too. The trouble is, that includes Napoleon himself, who, when he was forty, existed at a different time from Napoleon when he was thirteen. So Napoleon is a fake copy of himself. To be more precise, he is a long series of fake copies of himself. Not only is he a fake, he is not even a very good fake, because he looked quite different at forty than he had done at thirteen. He would not fool anybody.

People, as they get older, are never very good copies of their earlier selves. After a certain age, parts begin to drop off, and wrinkles begin to appear where there were no wrinkles in the original (or, if you live in America, parts are added on where there were no parts before). Of course reincarnated people are not physical copies at all, and the three hundred reborn Napoleons look nothing like Napoleon. Quite a large number of them are women, as it happens. So it looks as though I can continue to be the same person even if my body changes considerably. Adding a few temporal gaps would not seem to make such a crucial difference. So reincarnation and resurrection, the change of bodies with physical and temporal gaps, seem to be at least logically possible.

But how can you know that one person is really the same as a person who used to exist some time ago, perhaps in a different body? Buddhists are the greatest experts at detecting reincarnations, as they have to find reincarnated lamas every few years to run their monasteries. They test candidates by seeing whether they recognize objects or places that dead lamas had known well. And they look out for especially wise words, good behaviour, and mental calm and mindfulness, which suggest an advanced spiritual state suitable for a dead lama.

Their appeal is to memories and to unusual mental dispositions suggesting wisdom, compassion, and controlled mindfulness. The interesting thing is that Buddhists specifically deny that there is any permanent self which endures through successive incarnations. What they are interested in is a succession of mental acts and events which, they believe, is the result of long and strenuous moral striving and mental training on the part of some past successions of mental events.

Does it really matter whose mental strivings caused the present set of mental events to exist? The idea is that the present succession does not just come into existence for no reason. It has a cause or a long series of causes. Those causes are not primarily physical causes. They are successive acts of attention and effort, of attending and intending, which have gradually built up a tendency to generate mental states of deep understanding and compassion for all beings. Such states do not just occur. They are brought about by intentional actions. Other chains of mental action have brought about states of ignorance and indifference to or even hatred of other sentient beings.

All chains of intentional action bring about states of increased or decreased understanding and empathy. To comprehend the nature of such states we need to comprehend how and why they have come into being, for they carry within themselves the causal history of their origin. My present understanding of the world is essentially an understanding that has been developed through a long succession of past acts of insight or obtuseness, and I do not fully understand what I am (my co-present consciousness) unless I understand how this consciousness has come to be.

As Proust, or someone very like Proust, might say, the reason I like the taste of little cakes like madeleines may be found in experiences in the past which lie in some deep recess of my memory. A full self-understanding would unlock that past succession of memories – which is no doubt why the Enlightened One, the Buddha, is said to have full recollection of his many lives.

So I do not just say, "Someone (it does not matter who) in the past meditated for forty years, and I am now reaping the benefits of that by being calm and collected." I say, "I am continuing a particular causal succession of mental acts and experiences, even though I have a different body and there has been a long temporal interval between the past succession and its present continuation." Someone can be Napoleon now, if their dispositions and mental states have in fact been caused by and continue in a different context the succession of mental acts which made up the inner mental life of Napoleon.

There could be three hundred incarnated Napoleons. But if there were, something would have gone wrong with the causal process. The reason we reject all these putative Napoleons is that they do not have the memories, thoughts, and intentions of the original Napoleon, and in addition they suffer from other behavioural and mental problems that render them subject to delusions. But if they were perfectly capable of ordering their own lives sensibly, and if they did remember things that only Napoleon could have known, we might begin to be impressed. It is because the evidence is not good enough that many people reject reincarnation or resurrection of the dead, not because it is a logical impossibility.

If, however, there were three hundred reincarnated Napoleons, we would have good reason to doubt the intelligibility of the causal processes of the universe. Whereas the life of Napoleon, insofar as it was the result of free and intentional mental acts, should have generated just one megalomaniac of militaristic and domineering disposition, it would instead have generated three hundred such unfortunate individuals. While that is logically possible, that would be morally unfair both to all the three hundred people who had to suffer because of the acts of just the one previous Napoleon and to everybody who had to put up with these incorrectly processed Napoleons.

The priority of the mental

Things can go wrong with the universe, and if they do go wrong, we will just have to put up with it. But if things do not go radically wrong, it makes sense to say that **I continue to be the same person if I have the same knowledge, memories, thoughts, dispositions, and intentions, even if there were spatial and temporal gaps between the person I used to be and the person I now am, and as long as there exists no other person now who is identical with me** (which would complicate, but not completely undermine, the story).

Such a possibility gives priority to the mental over the physical or bodily. It denies the necessity of having some continuing identical substance to join two sets of conscious events together. And it places enormous importance on the conscious free intentions and efforts of sentient beings, which will affect the future in fundamental ways. It allows for the possibility of reincarnation or of other forms of life after bodily death. But of course its cogency depends upon there really being the sort of mental causality that the theory posits, and that is not at all obvious.

Whether or not we accept the possibility of reincarnation or resurrection (though it is difficult to dismiss them as absolutely impossible), we can hold that at least in this life chains of mental causality are normally (and perhaps always) mediated through temporally continuous physical bodies. This takes account of the fact that fully free intentional acts are probably much rarer in human life than we think. Most of our acts may well be the result of physical hard-wiring and habits established over millennia of evolutionary trial and error. Most of our characters and dispositions may well be due to the adventitious mixing of our parents' DNA, rather than to purely mental causes in the life of some person in the past. So while mental effort does have real effects on our mental life, and while that is of the utmost moral importance, humans are also socially and physically embodied and are subject to physical chains of causality that make any direct causal link between some past life and a present life very difficult to establish. Conscious intention is only one part, though morally by far the most important, of that complex of elements which goes to form a complete human person.

Part of the moral lesson here is that we should never say of some poor or relatively disabled person that it is "their fault" they are that way, because it must be due to something wrong they did in some past life. If that were so, we would expect that all millionaires would be past saints and all paupers would be past serial killers. Without trying to be too judgmental, that does not look quite right.

The conclusion of this Napoleonic episode is that we might agree that the world is made up of successions of events and acts, of processes, ordered in accordance with complex causal laws. Yet in the case of human persons these successions fall into distinct groups of cumulative subjective experiences. And a fairly clear way of distinguishing one such group is to say that, since its parts are subjective experiences, they are the experiences of one common subject of experiences, the "subject" being constituted precisely by that unique unity which binds these experiences together in one succession.

We might also agree that mental acts are very important parts of such processes, and that mental acts are different from passive objects or states and from purely physical or material events. Mental acts, unlike physical acts, normally form successions of causally related private experiences and intentions which work out progressively over time. Constantly renewed mental discipline and effort, attention and intention, result in states of mind and in actions that otherwise would not have existed.

Just as there is one "subject" of experiences, which binds them together in a uniquely subjective way, so we can say that there is one creative causal agent that continues to act over time through a succession of experiences. As long as we do not say that this subject and agent of experiences and actions exists separately and quite apart from the flow of events that constitute the life of the mind, it looks as though a "Cartesian" view of mental substance (as the subject of experiences and acts) is not in opposition to a process view of personal life. In fact, it is the concept of a continuing mental substance, rightly understood, that enables us to distinguish different sets of mental events from each other, and to see mental events as (at least in part) cumulatively and intentionally built up over time.

This is the very opposite of Ryle's concept of mind, because it privileges private states over publicly observable ones, yet it seems to follow from a consideration of what is morally important about personal identity.

Chapter Six

The place of human minds in the cosmos

It is important to stress (as Descartes mostly did) that human minds are fully integrated into an evolving material universe and do not inhabit some separate mental world. This very naturally leads to seeing the universe as a purposive process aimed at the progressive realization of intrinsic and objective values in and by finite minds within the universe. Human persons have a positive and responsible role to play within this process, so they are integrated into a material, bodily context and that is their proper environment.

I have argued that the mental is of primary importance in human personhood, but I am in no doubt that in humans the mental and the physical are mixed together in a closely integrated way, and both are implicated in the causal network that drives the world into the future. The problem is to say what this integration is. Whitehead's solution, shared by many philosophically minded scientists, is to say that the mental is the inner life of the physical. All physical phenomena have an inner or "private" aspect, in addition to what can be observed by public perception.

There are process thinkers, like Charles Hartshorne, who have argued that even electrons have free will, and they decide when to jump from one orbit to another within the atom. But it is hard to see why they should jump at one time rather than another or what the point of jumping is anyway. Intelligent consciousness as we know it does seem to depend on the very complex structure of brains, and on the interaction of millions of neurons. Electrons have no complex structure, and they seem to have rather limited opportunities for personal development or for really interesting and adventurous choices.

Nevertheless, it can seem plausible to think that consciousness cannot just arise out of nowhere, and be joined onto a brain in a completely accidental and unpredictable way. For many scientists it makes more sense to see consciousness as a natural development out of simpler elements, as an unfolding of potentialities inherent in matter from the first. Consciousness is the phenomenal appearing of things, together with thoughts that interpret those appearances. So maybe even the simplest sorts of things have some sort of phenomenal appearing (some way in which objects are represented), and some sort of interpretative or at least subjective reaction to such appearing. That is certainly what Whitehead thinks.

We do not have to be committed to the rather elaborate edifice of process philosophy to be attracted to this way of seeing consciousness as a natural development of simpler properties inherent in all material things. Philosophers like Rom Harre of Oxford and scientists like John Polkinghorne of Cambridge accept a very similar view. That is to say, as well as their publicly observable appearance, the basic elements of matter have an inner structure that is not publicly observable, but that drives their causal route through space-time. Materialists (Theory 3) might even say as much, at least insofar as they accept that many forms of material reality (at the subatomic level, for instance) are inaccessible to sense-observation. But materialists wish to remove any even embryonic hint of consciousness, value or purpose from matter. Epiphenomenalists (Theory 5) accept that consciousness emerges from matter, but they typically deny that minds could possibly exist without matter, and that minds have any real causal role to play in the cosmos. So again minds have to emerge by accident, or unintentionally, from a material universe without consciousness or purpose.

Idealist philosophers do not usually think that there are little fully conscious minds driving atoms around. But they do think that even "material" processes are not totally random, directionless, mechanistic or wholly determined by absolute and arbitrary laws. Purpose or teleology may be built into nature from the first. The material universe is perhaps more like an organism than like a repetitive machine. Whereas an older generation of scientists and philosophers thought the universe was rather like a watch, many now regard the universe as more like a large organism. It grows and develops, and its first stages can only be properly understood when its completely developed state is perceived.

A human embryo does not unexpectedly and accidentally become an adult person, and it can only be properly understood as a potential adult. So we might think that the primitive elements – be they quarks or superstrings or something as yet undiscovered – of the universe do not unexpectedly clump into atoms, which surprisingly form molecules, which accidentally generate proteins, which unforeseeably build organisms, which by pure chance produce brains and societies of organic beings, so that the whole present universe is a totally unexpected accident. On the organic view, this trajectory of development, of increasingly integrated complexity, producing new sorts of properties, and eventually the ability to comprehend and consciously shape the future of the universe, is implicit in the universe at the moment of the Big Bang or in whatever gives rise to that primordial explosion.

From this point of view, it is a basic mistake of reductive

materialism to try to explain everything in terms of its simplest elements – as though a large enough group of such simple elements just had to be mixed up at random for a long time, and would then produce brains, thoughts, and the theory of relativity. The main alternative to such reductionism is holistic explanation. Simple elements are explained in terms of the wholes of which they are constituent parts, and of the fullest realization of all the possibilities of a dynamic and developing system.

It remains a deep mystery how a fully realized society of intelligent and purposive agents (which is what we actually have in this corner of the universe) can be potential in the simple state of infinite density and mass which was the Big Bang. But it may be helpful to think of the space-time universe, not just as a set of separate parts, but as a completed whole.

The universe does not consist of discrete temporal slices, all isolated in their own little bubbles of time. Causal tracks and connections extend back and forward through time, and a present moment of consciousness can contain echoes of the past and premonitions or anticipations of the future. So we might see the universe not as a set of atomistic time-slices accidentally stuck together, but as one interconnected or entangled space-time whole. We do not see what objects are by seeing just one temporal slice of their existence. That would be like trying to understand a person by looking hard at them when they are asleep. We need to see them from beginning to end of their temporal existence and within the whole context in which they exist.

An "object" is what physicists call a world-line in space-time. The early stages of its temporal existence are properly seen as parts of a whole world-line which adequately describe the object only when it is seen as a whole. Albert Einstein thought that the whole of time, with all its constituent world-lines, actually exists, from the first moment to the last. We only seem to move through it one moment at a time. In reality both our past and our future are timelessly existent and never come into being or pass away. He apparently found great consolation in the fact that his dead friends were not really non-existent. They all exist timelessly, and they only seem to be dead to the rest of us.

I suspect that you would have to be a very advanced mathematical physicist to be consoled by the thought that dead people all really exist, because time is an illusion. Most of us will continue to be more impressed by the thought that we will never meet them again in time. Even if in some strange way we could meet them outside time, we would still not be able to talk to them, since talking takes time, and if there was no time, there would be no time for a good conversation. We would just have to stare at each other, frozen in changeless immobility. That might be all right for Einstein, but it would be very frustrating for most people, especially for the talkative ones.

A "supernatural" origin for the cosmos

Whether the passing of time is real or not, it might be just wrong to think that at the moment of the Big Bang nothing existed except a very simple physical state of infinite density. Most cosmologists suppose that there would also have been a whole set of quantum laws, and perhaps those very complex and precise balances of energy that would constitute what is called a "quantum vacuum". In modern cosmology, there is something outside space-time, from which space-time originates, which has a rich mathematical structure. There is, in other words, a "supernatural" reality; a more fundamental layer of reality beyond space-time.

Materialists are really shocked at this turn of events. Some of them simply ignore it and say that it is not really science. David Hume held that it was absurd to think that the puny human mind could speculate about the "origin of worlds", when nobody had ever observed such things. Nevertheless, there are chairs of this "absurdity" in most major Western universities.

What is that supernatural reality like? Some think that at least the basic laws and principles that existed at the beginning of the universe must have been very simple – largely because, they think, if we are going to explain the origin of the universe, the explanation will have to be simpler than what it explains or it will not be an explanation.

This, however, is plainly false. It is doubtful if it even makes sense. Quantum field theory explains the behaviour of events in a particle accelerator. But in what sense is quantum theory "simpler" than very small things smashing into one another at immense speeds in a large hollow tube? Of course it is nice to have an elegant and simple theory if it does the same work as an ugly and complicated one. But the important thing about a scientific theory is that it produces general equations from which the behaviour of physical particles can be predicted. If those equations turn out to be complex – and they are already so complex that very few people can even understand them – that is life!

We have no right to expect that there will be stateable equations that govern all physical behaviour or that they will be simple and elegant – though we have been very lucky to find there are many such equations (like Newton's laws of motion). We are in no position to lay it down as a necessary truth that there will be simple elegant laws to explain the Big Bang. What we need are laws and principles that will explain the whole space-time structure of the universe, not just some initial state of the universe – which may turn out to be the least interesting thing in the universe, except insofar as it is the starting-point for the whole cosmic story.

There might, then, be laws that help to explain how and why this universe was generated 13.7 billion years ago, in terms of the much later realization of complex states that were only implicit in the first state of the universe. Such laws would set out a direction of development, culminating in a completion of initial potencies, a set of possible goals that can be seen as fulfilments of tendencies inherent in the universe itself.

A goal is a future state that is rationally choosable by an intelligent conscious being. A fully intelligent conscious being is one that would choose states that are intrinsically worthwhile – good just for their own sake and not for any other reason. If anything is ever worth choosing, then there must be some states that are intrinsically worthwhile. If we try to think of the sorts of goals for a universe that could be rationally choosable, we might think of such things as the ability of a material universe to come to understand and shape its own being and to generate communities of organisms that can themselves, as Aristotle put it, find happiness in the pursuit of states and processes that are worthwhile for their own sake.

We might think of a universe generating beings with conscious capacities such as those for creativity, understanding, appreciation, and free relationship. If this might indeed be the fullest flourishing of the cosmic organism, then the initial laws of the universe will render it inevitable that this, or some very similar, cosmic organism will exist and will come into full bloom before, like all organisms, it decays and dies. The initial laws will, in that case, not simply exist without any point or purpose. They will have a good reason for existing – the reason being precisely the generation of intrinsically worthwhile states that can be known, appreciated, and produced by intelligent agents. The initial laws will be, in other words, purposive or goal-directed. Purpose has been ejected from scientific explanations for almost four hundred years. Perhaps, in modern cosmology and in idealist philosophy, it is making a comeback.

What I have tried to do in this chapter is to suggest how conscious personal life and the material structure of the universe fit together in a coherent way if we suppose that the physical universe has the purpose of producing personal consciousness as the natural realization of its inherent and original capacities. Consciousness is not just an alien substance injected into the material universe at an arbitrary point – a picture which Cartesian dualism, if interpreted unkindly, may suggest. Rather, consciousness results from the natural generation of capacities inherent in the structure of matter itself, as it develops forms of organized complexity over time. A picture of cosmic evolution that portrays responsible and intelligent minds as a natural, possibly inevitable, outcome of the growth of an organic material universe could be the key to understanding how spirit and flesh, mind and matter, soul and body, can be integrally intertwined, and yet how the primacy of spirit, as the ultimate purposive driving force of an evolving universe, can be maintained.

Could the universe have a goal?

All this could be seen of course as a piece of human arrogance. Those values of creativity, understanding, and so on – are they not just the preferences of a small number of rather prissy human beings, projected improbably onto the universe? If you walk into your local bar and say, "What I'm looking for is creativity, understanding, appreciation, and free relationship," the odds are that everybody will ostentatiously look the other way. With luck, somebody might say, "Well we have darts, and we can probably find some dominoes if you like. How about some pickled eggs?"

Is it really plausible to think that the universe, so vast in extent, exists just to produce beings like us? Did it really take 13.7 billion years just to produce *Big Brother* and the Wimbledon Tennis Championships? There aren't, it may be said, any universal or cosmic values. There are just things that people in bars, bus queues, shopping malls, and offices happen to like at the time. And that hardly seems grand enough to merit the title of the goal of the cosmic process, the ultimate reason for the Big Bang. Or would you really want to say that the answer to the question "Why does the universe exist?" is "So that I can enjoy a pint of beer"?

Actually, you might. Some physicists have estimated that, starting from the initial Big Bang, and allowing the known laws of nature to take their course and gradually build up heavy atoms, complex molecules, and central nervous systems, the emergence of intelligent carbon-based life-forms would have taken about 13.7 billion years. Since the Big Bang, the universe has been expanding as fast as it can, so that by now it extends for billions of light-years. Therefore, the reason there is so much empty space around is that it has to exist in order to produce me (assuming that I am a pretty good example of an intelligent life-form. I am certainly a good example of a beer-drinking life-form).

It seems that I am much more important to the universe than you might think. Or if you think I am a rather disappointing specimen, hardly worth 13.7 billion years of effort, you could say that at least intelligent life is worth having, and if it takes billions of years to produce it, does that really matter? The process itself is not pointless; it is not just a means to an end. It has immense beauty and elegance, and it is worthwhile for its own sake. But that beauty and elegance can only be appreciated when conscious life-forms come into existence (unless there were consciousnesses existing outside the universe, which could appreciate its development).

We should not think that it took the birth and death of millions of star-systems and the extermination of millions of now extinct organisms, just to produce one man drinking beer in a pub. However, in one sense that man is more valuable than all those galaxies, because there was no one to appreciate their beauty, whereas at least he enjoys his pint. The greatest beauty that passes unknown and unappreciated is in one sense of less value than the enjoyment of a pint of beer, just because there is no one to put a value on that beauty. There is no one who values it, and so in a real sense it has no value – until it is known and appreciated for what it is. There are no actual values unless someone values them. So consciousness is necessary for there to be any actual values in the universe.

Still, I do not suppose anyone but Homer Simpson would think that drinking beer is the greatest value in the universe. Maybe humans are just one small primitive part of cosmic history. What would be really impressive as a goal for the universe would be the genesis of a consciousness, or perhaps a society of consciousnesses, that understood and could control the cosmos itself, which could devise endless creative purposes and experience unlimited types and intensities of feeling. That such an existence would be of value is not just a projection of a few arbitrary human likes and dislikes onto the universe. It is a goal, a desirable state, which any conscious intelligent being would choose, whether it drank beer or not. It might prefer beer in its present state, but it could at least see, when sober, that a really intelligent being would choose the goal of a cosmic consciousness that could be endlessly creative and that could experience infinite states of enjoyment and beauty – and then it could have endless kinds of beer whenever it wanted, without any of the ill-effects that beer usually has.

If we can see humans as only the beginning of the development of intelligent consciousness in the universe, consciousness that will exist for untold billions of years, then it makes more sense to see the long development of cosmic evolution as oriented toward a worthwhile goal. We may think we exist on the last half-page of the many-volume book that is the history of the universe. But if there are even more volumes still to come, that changes the picture entirely. Admittedly this is speculative. It is a sort of ideal utopianism, constructed by thinking what things would be like if there really were ultimately worthwhile goals for the universe that all fully informed intelligent beings would desire. Things might not be like that, though I rather hope they are.

Idealists need not be committed to such a utopian and ultra-optimistic idea. In the Indian traditions there is an infinite series of universes, each of which eventually ends with an age of increasing chaos and evil (a *Kali Yuga*). The goals of the cosmos are realized only beyond the cosmos, either in absorption into the Supreme Self or in some spiritual realm rather like Western ideas of paradise. Even Hegel, though he remained typically ambiguous, speculated that the final goal of "reconciliation with Absolute Spirit" might not exist in this physical cosmos. And Whitehead explicitly denies that there is any realizable final goal of the universe.

Whitehead thinks of the basic directional laws of the cosmos and the states to which they lead as primordial "aims": a timeless set of possible goals and of possible tracks to realizing them in many ways and in many forms. He does not think of there being just one final consummating and unsurpassable state. He certainly does not think that human life is it. He rather thinks of the process of creativity as being unending. It is also always compromised by conflict between different organic forms that pursue different aims, and by the fact that some aims will be so limited as to be destructive rather than creative.

Whichever of these varieties of idealism we prefer, for all of them chance, impersonal laws of nature, and creative freedom play an important part in the complex processes of the universe. There may be no final perfection for the universe. Its tendency toward truth, beauty, and goodness is real, but may be always qualified by the existence of elements which resist that tendency, though they too are parts of the cosmic structure. This may be thought of as a modern version of the world of Platonic "forms" being imperfectly realized in the material world, though it differs by stressing the importance of time and of evolutionary development, thereby giving the universe a history of which Plato could scarcely have conceived.

Chapter Seven

Dual–aspect idealism

If there is purposive causality in the universe, it will obviously make an enormous difference to what happens. Events will not occur just by chance or accident, but the whole universe will be directed toward the existence of persons and the realization of personal values. Since the natural sciences normally set aside questions of value, they cannot as such establish whether the universe is directed toward the existence of specific values or not. But the findings of the natural sciences are certainly relevant to the question of whether there is direction or progress of any sort in the observed universe. It seems to me that it is a reasonable hypothesis that there is. If so, this helps to confirm the form of idealism I am defending, which could be called dual-aspect idealism, because it stresses the importance of the material aspect as a means of allowing the potentialities of mind to be expressed.

Many modern evolutionary theorists are so opposed to the notion of direction and purpose in cosmic history that they insist on stressing the totally fortuitous and random nature of biological evolution. This is rather odd, because they mostly also think that the basic laws of physics are not at all fortuitous and random. Indeed, many of them are physical determinists and think that at a physical level things must obey the laws of nature and could not be other than they actually are. This is the opposite of randomness!

There seem to be four main reasons for this resistance to directionality. First, there is too much waste and suffering in evolution for it to be planned. Second, many organisms like bacteria do not evolve, but stay happily as they are, so there does not seem to be a "universal striving" in evolution. Third, the evolution of humans depends on a number of freak accidents, like the meteor impact that may have destroyed the dinosaurs and other disasters that turned out well for humans but rather badly for every other form of life. And fourth, the mechanisms of Darwinian evolution, random mutation and natural selection, do not seem to allow for any sort of intelligent or purposive selection. Ideas of direction or purpose smack too much of "vitalism", the exploded view that there is some sort of "life force" at work in addition to natural mechanisms in evolution.

This is precisely where basic philosophical beliefs influence what are supposed to be strictly scientific theories. I am not against such influence. On the contrary I am all for it. But in my opinion this is the wrong influence from a false philosophical theory – or at the very least, from a highly disputed one.

These arguments of evolutionary naturalism can be very easily dismissed. In response to the first argument, we can say that talk of waste and suffering is completely irrelevant to the question of whether there is direction in evolution. If there is a direction, it is from simplicity to complexity, from unconsciousness to consciousness, from lack of any appreciation of value to the understanding and appreciation of many moral, intellectual, and aesthetic values, and from chance and necessity to intelligent purpose. We can observe this progress in the evolution of human beings from unconscious and unintelligent stardust.

There is no reason why such a progress should be without blind alleys and eddies which do not lead in the requisite direction, as long as the process as a whole inevitably leads to the "higher" states. In fact, one rational structure for such progress is a system which generates a number of alternative possible tracks, where all possibilities are tried and only some lead to cumulative progressive tracks. That may lead to waste and suffering, but that does not make the structure less rational.

In response to the second argument, it is not at all necessary that every item in the structure should be seeking to mutate in a positive direction. Indeed, it is necessary that most items should not mutate, but should preserve their structure, to provide a solid base on which new mutations can be built. The structure must provide, therefore, for the repetition of dependable elements, with mutations that do not lead to great structural changes. But some, perhaps a small number, relatively speaking, of mutations must lead to structural changes – and that is what we see.

What about the third argument, stressing the role of genuine accident in the evolutionary process? Quantum physics is usually taken to undermine a wholly deterministic interpretation of the laws of nature. But of course it does not undermine the fact that there are laws of nature. What it suggests is that the laws will in general produce predictable results, but at the subatomic level we will have to work with probabilities where not all details are predictable – and sometimes this will result in larger scale unpredictabilities. In other words, there are elements of genuine randomness, but even they are governed by laws of probability, and most probabilities cancel out at higher levels to leave the inevitability of the general processes of nature intact. Only occasionally, and usually at times not directly observable by humans, will genuine alternatives at the macro level appear. But some of those occasions might have decisive and dramatic consequences.

It is also a generally accepted rule of quantum physics that physical phenomena are entangled, so that basic physical elements affect one another in non-local ways, and no phenomenon can be considered totally in isolation from other phenomena in the universe. This fact also places constraints on what possibilities are open within the system. As Michio Kaku says, "Einstein often asked himself whether God had any choice in creating the universe. According to superstring theorists, once we demand a unification of quantum theory and general relativity, God had no choice."[1] This is a rather picturesque way of saying that if there are going to be intelligent carbon-based organisms in the universe, then the general structure of the universe, including some of its unpleasant features, could not have been other than it is.

The limits of human observation mean that we are unlikely ever to know in detail what the necessary constraints on the universe are. We cannot observe the whole universe every time we want to assess the probability of an event occurring, and so we will never know all the laws and constraints that govern the occurrence of any event, much less the structure of the whole universe.

Suppose, then, as a general hypothesis, that there is a basic teleology in nature: a dynamic process, involving elements of chance and also a large element of repetitive law-like behaviour, nevertheless ensures that specific "developed" states will inevitably be realized in the cosmic process. This is not the idea of some sort of person interfering in the process from outside. It is the idea that the process itself has inherent direction and goal, set by the fundamental and timeless laws of the cosmos. The existence of such a teleology will make a difference to specific events that occur, for it is part of the laws of nature, not an interference with them.

The demise of the dinosaurs

When an astronomer says that the formation of planet earth and the genesis of organic life on its surface was the result of a fantastic series of hugely improbable events, this has to be seen in the light of the fact that the cosmos may be set up inevitably to realize organic life forms. In that light it is not at all improbable that events conducive to the genesis of life should occur, though the presence of chance elements does mean that some events destructive of life and purpose will also occur.

The choice, in other words, is not between perfect design and complete chance. It seems more likely that the cosmos moves inevitably toward intelligent consciousness through a partly free (and because free, partly undetermined and therefore partly random) and partly determined (because otherwise there would be no reliable structure) creative process of trial and error.

There was nobody who specifically planned that a meteor should be dispatched to exterminate the dinosaurs 65 million years ago (assuming that it was a meteor that wiped out the dinosaurs) and open the way for humans to evolve. But it may not have been just a by-product, unfortunate for dinosaurs, of totally blind forces of nature. Dinosaurs, after all, flourished for many millions of years. They had their day in the sun, and perhaps they existed for much longer than humans may. But they did not seem to be going anywhere, and they probably ate anything that looked as if it might be going somewhere. They were blocking the evolutionary development of the universe. They were, to put it bluntly, a creative experiment that had run out of steam. To put it more kindly, the process had succeeded in producing impressively large reptiles, but they had reached a dead end. If they had got any larger, their brains would no longer have been able to communicate with their legs in time to run after their prey.

We may think of the destruction of the dinosaurs as a state that presented itself as possible but not inevitable on one of those relatively rare occasions when decisive selections between options are likely. What is required to make sense of this is to think of present situations as containing a number of alternative futures. There will be many constraints on which alternatives can be selected, and on which of them might have decisive consequences. But one causal factor in these complex situations, idealists think, will be the general teleological tendency of the cosmos. This of course will be too much for materialists, who have a paranoid fear of any causal factors in addition to the "blind" laws of nature.

Even materialists have to admit, however, that according to quantum theory there can be alternative futures, and that we do not know the causal principles that select between them. Materialists can always say that these alternatives cancel out on the molecular scale, that purely Darwinian principles are quite sufficient to explain all evolutionary changes, and that anyway there are no "mystical" non-Darwinian principles, so there! This is the fourth argument that sceptics about purpose often produce.

An appropriate reply is that quantum indeterminacies do not always cancel out, and they may in the right conditions amplify into major changes (as with the "butterfly effect", which keeps weather forecasters in a job even when they get everything wrong). Indeterminacy may not be confined to the subatomic world. Quantum theory has shown that physics does not have to adopt a wholly deterministic view of nature. So there may be indeterminacies – that is, alternative futures without one of them being wholly determined by physical events in the past – at many points in the physical world. Unless we adopt the dogma that the laws of nature have to determine the future in only one way, an element of indeterminism in nature seems very likely. Why should universal laws completely determine everything that happens?

Specifically, the intentions of conscious beings may help to decide what happens in the future of the universe, and such intentions, being mental and not physical, may be in principle unpredictable and not wholly determined by previous physical events. Any scientist who says we know all the causal principles there are, and that those principles are sufficient to determine everything that happens, is not being wholly honest. So there is plenty of room in our universe for events that are influenced not just by general laws of nature, but by conscious goals and intentions. There may be general teleological principles built into nature which will help to explain the apparent direction of evolutionary change toward intelligent consciousness and the fully purposive direction of events.

When someone resorts to saying, "This event was just an

extremely improbable occurrence," we need to remember that science is in the business of making the apparently improbable less improbable. If we cannot do so, that is a defeat for Darwinian theory, not a success! Teleological explanation would render the extinction of the dinosaurs more likely than it would otherwise have been – always assuming that small mammals were more likely to evolve intelligence than T. Rex was. So while dinosaurs may not like the thought that they were holding up the progress of cosmic evolution, it could be the case that their extinction, while not specifically planned by a dinosaur-hating God, was not wholly an unpredictable accident. Sooner or later they would have been replaced, and the proximity of a meteor provided one way in which this could occur, naturally though not inevitably.

I conclude that modern evolutionary theory, when it is not infected by materialist philosophy, does allow for direction or purpose in the cosmic process. It compels us to include a place for chance in the process, but when combined with physics it sets the operation of chance within limits that are imposed by the fundamental laws and constants of the physical world. That is just what seems to be required for the generation of stable and yet limitedly free intelligent persons. To that extent, evolutionary science, especially when set in the context of a general evolutionary cosmology, is wholly consonant with the hypothesis that there is a goal for the material cosmos.

Purposive explanation and idealist thought

But is teleological explanation scientific? Final causality was ruled out of science in the seventeenth century, as appealing but fruitless and obstructive – "like vestal virgins", Francis Bacon said. Contemporary science does not deal with purposes in nature. That does not mean there are none. Contemporary science does not deal with the taste of tomato soup either, but there is one. So perhaps purposive explanation exists, but is not part of modern science.

There is a good reason why not. If you are going to talk about purpose, you have to talk about the goal at which a purpose aims. Then you have to evaluate that goal as good – nobody aims at something because they regard it as bad. Even masochists, who repeatedly harm themselves, are doing so because (to take just one possibility) they think they deserve it, and it is good to get one's just deserts – and probably also because they get a sense of sexual pleasure out of it. Some people have very unusual desires. But I am not going to go there.

The point is that science tries to discount personal evaluations. It tries not to say whether something is good or bad, but to give a neutral description of what happens. It is therefore not the job of science to talk about worthwhile goals, and that stops it from talking about purposes. Teleological explanation does talk about worthwhile goals, and supposes that cosmic processes may be directed to achieving them. But purely descriptive science cannot say what those goals are or use the fact that processes seem to be directed to attain them in order to construct mathematical equations that give predictions that can be publicly tested. Aiming at goals is too infected by creativity and freedom to be captured in mathematically exact predictions. So it is not part of modern natural science.

Teleological explanation, in short, belongs to philosophy, not to science. Ah, materialists may say, so it is just a matter of personal opinion? Indeed it is, just like materialism. None of us can avoid taking up a philosophical position, if we think hard enough. That is very irritating, if you dislike philosophy and think it a waste of time.

The basic motivation for positing teleological explanation starts from an analysis of human experience. We have purposes and we act intentionally. Then it proceeds to probe the nature of the world as it is experienced by us and finds (perhaps!) that it is an appearance of a veiled and mysterious reality, not accessible to sense-observation. It discovers the positive activity of thought in constructing the world of appearances and so posits that constructive thinking is part of reality as it is in itself. Constructive thinking is intentional; it is freely aimed at the goal of understanding the world. So teleological (intentional) explanation is part of the real world. It is at that point that we may be led to ask whether we can find traces of it in the observed world of appearances and in the general structure of that world rather than just in human experience.

Since materialism has been abandoned at the very beginning of this process, there is no reason to exclude teleology in principle from the general structure of nature. It is a viable option. When we ask how consciousness originates very late in the history of a universe that begins with a Bang, it can become a compelling thought that it is not a total surprise, but a natural realization of the initial potency of matter itself. So now we look for some more primitive states that can naturally give rise to finite consciousnesses through a long emergent process, and idealist philosophy begins.

Dual-aspect idealism – the truth at last?

The basic laws that structure the universe do not have to be merely mechanical principles with no inkling of the consequences of these mechanical motions. They may include possible goals and processes of value and the future genesis of consciousness as the fruition of matter itself. One way to think about this is to imagine, as some mathematicians do, an abstract space of possibilities, laying down future tracks to future goals and determining, with much room for individual creativity, how the universe will proceed. The actual goals and tracks that are "chosen" may depend on many factors, but evolutionary views of the cosmos suggest that there will be an emergent and developmental process in which finite parts of the cosmos become more and more capable of envisaging and pursuing their own creative paths.

It is consistent with modern quantum theory to regard the whole cosmos as a web of interacting energies, of spatially and temporally located powers. Each part is not, like Leibniz's unfortunate monads, isolated and closed in on itself. Each part is essentially open to the totality of the space-time nexus. Each receives stimuli from all the others that surround it, integrates those stimuli into a unity of being, and actively responds in accordance with its own specific powers. At the simplest level, for instance that of subatomic wave-particles, both stimuli and responses are more or less algorithmic – they behave in accordance with regular and largely predictable routines, described by the basic forces of nature like electromagnetism, gravity, and nuclear forces. Only in this way can they form stable atoms upon which more complex unities can come to exist.

As atoms form into molecules and they in turn form long chains of RNA and DNA, patterns of stimulus, integration, and response grow more complex. Primitive sentience is a function of complex organic forms, which increasingly act as individuals, though they essentially function as parts of a larger integrated whole.

Probably at the point when brains begin to exist, there is a radically new form of complexity, for which stimuli are registered with intensities of feeling and responded to with some creative agency. In human beings, the most complex form known to us, the conceptual or interpretative element predominates, and responsive actions become subject to causality by envisaged outcomes (intention). The sense of a continuing and active self emerges, interpreting the stimuli received from "outside" as appearances of a world of objects, and intending to modify those objects in accordance with consciously formed purposes.

Humans have private perspectives on, feelings for, and thoughts about, phenomena interpreted as expressions or mediations of external objects (including other persons). They express such feelings and thoughts in external ways, like language. But humans know that language or physical gesture may conceal inner thoughts or fail to state them adequately or be interpreted in many ways, some of them quite mistaken, by those who perceive only the observed expressions. Thus each thought or feeling is known in two ways – as expressed physically and as experienced internally.

It is important to note that the physical expression is itself in a sense an "internal perception" of some observer, a subjective appearance of something taken to be objective, though it does not exist objectively as it appears to the observer. In that sense, the conscious event has logical priority and primary importance, though it is natural to see it as emerging from a long process of physical development.

In the first four chapters of this book I argued for a general philosophical position somewhere between dualism and idealism, and suggested that some form of dualism and some form of idealism probably converged on an acceptable view. That would mean that matter would not merely be an illusion or a content of some mind or minds, but would have its own form of reality. Yet matter would ultimately depend for its existence on a mind-like reality.

A pressing problem for modern philosophy is how to relate matter and mind in a satisfactory way. An evolutionary view would find much to resonate with in Whitehead's view of the world as a succession of transitory events, each of which has an "inner" aspect as well as an outward physical appearance. For idealists, that inner aspect is the causal driving force of a cumulative and creative process of increasing organized complexity, generating richer forms of consciousness and purposive causality.

I call this a form of idealism because the engine of the process is not the mechanical movements of non-purposive physical entities, but the potentially mind-like reality or realities that are creatively and progressively expressed in the physical cosmos, and in the gradual unfolding of values that were implicit from the first in that cosmos. It is sometimes, however, called monism, because it insists that "feelings" (the inner aspect) and matter are bound together as aspects of a unitary reality. I argued that this is actually identical with a form of dualism that sees mind as the individuating agent of the unity and cumulative development of different streams of individual consciousness and purposive agency, but which allows that such streams of consciousness are firmly embodied in (bound together with) a physical cosmos.

It may seem confusing to mix idealism, monism, and dualism in this way. But perhaps what that shows is that we should not pour our theories too strictly into neatly labelled jars. What I am suggesting is a form of qualified absolute idealism. It could be called dual-aspect idealism. I do not mind the name, as long as it is clear that I mean to argue in favour of two hypotheses. First, that the most important feature of human persons is that they are streams or chains of mental acts and events, streams that are distinguished from one another by each containing experiences of one and only one uniting and cumulatively shaping subject. Second, that these streams of consciousness are the inner aspects of complex organized physical systems, with a long evolutionary history and an inherent potentiality for generating and realizing consciously created and appreciated values.

This provides a general picture of what human persons are that I think is philosophically plausible and consistent with the best modern science. Yet it is undoubtedly the case that many people feel that any sort of dualism or idealism, even or perhaps especially a dual-aspect idealism, is somehow incompatible with contemporary science. This is my cue to return to the work of Gilbert Ryle and re-examine why he thought Cartesian dualism was a myth. It may be that Ryle actually helped to invent the myth, and that Ryle's own account is capable of a much more idealistic interpretation than he ever dreamed. Of course Professor Ryle never actually had any dreams, since such things are private events, which do not, he thought, exist. So I will have to dream for him.

Chapter Eight

Metaphysics and common-sense philosophy

Gilbert Ryle's arguments aim to undermine both dualism and idealism. In the rest of this book, I seek to assess just how strong his arguments really are. It is necessary first of all, however, to examine Ryle's general view of philosophy. For he thought that metaphysics, in the sense of a general theory of the nature of reality, is a fairly useless or even impossible undertaking. That would make my project superfluous. I try to show that no thinking person can really escape some sort of metaphysics (some theory of what kinds of things really exist), and that Ryle himself actually had one, which was some sort of common-sense (or ordinary language) philosophy. So the question of metaphysics is important and unavoidable – and I think the reason why many people are materialists is that they do not take the metaphysical question seriously enough.

I may seem to have come a long way from Ryle's *The Concept of Mind*. But the point has been to see how Ryle's denial of inner processes is almost the exact opposite of the idealist claim that it is just such inner processes, culminating in intelligent consciousness, that form the core and the inherent teleological aim of reality.

Most of our ideas and beliefs are pretty much determined by the very first steps of thought we take. Ryle starts *The Concept of Mind* with a set of philosophical assumptions or premises that are going to guide everything else he says. What I have been trying to do is to show that those premises are far from obviously true. For lots of philosophers, they are obviously false. Only if you accept them as true will the rest of Ryle's book seem convincing – in fact, it will come to seem pretty obvious, and we might wonder why nobody thought of it before.

But you can get out of Ryle's system by rejecting his first assumptions. What I have done is to set out some alternative assumptions that other philosophers make. There are living philosophers who still follow each of the alternatives that I have outlined. I myself am convinced that some version of idealism is true, and I am attracted to some key ideas of process philosophy. I am pretty sure that materialism is false.

Philosophy, it must be said, is not good for decisiveness. If you have a reasonably open mind, you will probably be persuaded by every new philosophy book you read – at least for a day or two. But as you get to know more and more theories, and you see all the good arguments philosophers can find for them, you get less and less able to decide which one is true. I once asked a very well known philosopher of religion whether he believed in God. "Well," he said, "as a Catholic I do, but as a Buddhist I don't." "But are you a Catholic or a Buddhist?" I rather foolishly asked. To which his reply was, "Sometimes." I suppose that in his Buddhist moods he could have quoted the Buddha and said, "I am and I am not, and it is not the case that either I am or that I am not." But that would not have been much better.

I actually find the indecisiveness of philosophy rather helpful.

Sometimes you just have to make decisions and stick by them. But it can be helpful to remember that we are rarely as certain as we think we are, and our own basic philosophical beliefs are rarely as obviously true as we pretend they are. Maybe the best we can do is to say which beliefs seem to us most obviously false and which seem most appealing, and admit that not everyone is going to agree with our decisions.

So I suppose the minimum thing I would say about Ryle is that his view is not as obviously true as he thinks it is – although it is not quite clear that he always thought it was obviously true. He did confess to me that on one occasion he thought he might have had a mental image. But then he recovered his composure and decided that he had only formed the belief that he had nearly had a mental image, without actually having nearly had one.

Gilbert Ryle was a common-sense philosopher – except that, because he was after all an Oxford man, he probably thought that only the members of Oxford Senior Common Rooms really possessed common sense. Most other people are superstitious and deluded most of the time. And that is the trouble with common sense. It is just not very common. What most common people think is mostly nonsense. But there is no system of philosophy that calls itself "common-nonsense" philosophy. At least the nonsense talked by philosophers is not common. And the common sense that philosophers share is very unlike what common people think.

Ryle was a leading member of a common-sense school that is sometimes called "ordinary-language philosophy". We must remember that this is Oxford ordinary language, and it uses words that most people have never heard of. Philosophers of this school do not try to find out exactly what common-sense beliefs might be. Instead they talk about how people actually use language. They do not of course actually go out onto the streets and listen to ordinary people talking. The unwritten union rules of British universities state that only sociologists are allowed to do that. What philosophers must do is to sit in armchairs and think about people talking.

It turns out that as long as these imaginary people keep talking, everything goes reasonably smoothly. But when they start to think about what they are saying, things go horribly wrong. Then they start to ask questions like, "What did I mean by what I just said?" But in order to answer this question they first have to know what they mean by meaning. As they cannot work this out, because they are not quite sure what the question means, what they say quickly becomes meaningless. And philosophy is born.

It is a bit like riding a bicycle. If you just keep peddling, you will get along nicely. But if you ask yourself exactly how you keep your balance, you will probably fall off while you are trying to work it out. Most philosophers are like cyclists who fall off their bicycles, because they cannot work out exactly how they manage to stay on them.

So the job of ordinary-language philosophers is to stop people asking philosophical questions. Wittgenstein, a leading exponent of this type of philosophy, though regrettably he was based at Cambridge, thought that it was ridiculous to claim to be a professional philosopher − it was equivalent to claiming to be a professor of nonsense and grammatical mistakes. Unfortunately he was a professional philosopher and so were many of his pupils. They remained sane, when they did, by claiming that all other philosophers were talking nonsense, but that they had seen through the nonsense, and their job was simply to stop people being deluded by philosophers. They largely succeeded and in consequence they have largely become extinct. There was nothing left for philosophers to do.

On trying not to have a philosophical theory

Ryle and Wittgenstein both wrote so beautifully and were such commanding personalities that this became a dominant form of **common-sense philosophy** in mid-twentieth century Britain. It is common-sense because it refuses to invent grand theories about the universe just as a result of sitting in an armchair and thinking, and it insists on the diversity and flexibility of language, not as a clue to the ultimate nature of reality, but as a natural expression of human social behaviour.

The killer question, however, is this: it is said that philosophical theories arise out of misinterpretations of language use. But isn't that a philosophical theory? It is, after all, an important insight that language has many different functions, that we learn it from others in a particular social context, and that a large part of its use is practical or action-guiding, not theoretical or descriptive. That is a view about what language is and about how it relates to the real world. It is a pragmatic theory, implying that the relation is one of usefulness, that there are many sorts of usefulness (depending on what we want it to be useful for), and that preferences and interests may well differ from one society, time, and place, to another.

This theory also claims that most traditional philosophical problems, like that of materialism versus idealism, determinism versus free will, passion versus reason or the subjectivity versus the objectivity of values, result from misinterpretations of language. I guess most philosophers who take one of these positions would be annoyed at being told they had merely made some kind of grammatical mistake. They think they are disagreeing about what is the case, even though with these sorts of question it does not seem possible to decide with certainty what the case is.

Philosophy deals with undecidable yet apparently factual questions, which sometimes have great practical consequences. One of those, which I spent some time on in earlier chapters, is whether observed objects remain the same when they are not observed. Ryle might say that is an unreal question, since it only arises in philosophy seminars, which can seem pretty unreal occasions. Professor Ayer, however, believed that the answer to that question was very important. Ayer agreed with the realists that what we see is what there is, but added that what there is is nothing except what we see. The idea of a world of unobserved physical objects is a logical construct, invented for pragmatic reasons – it helps us to find our way around the world if we pretend that it is really there.

But if we realize that it is not really there, we will see that there is no point in talking about it or in discussing its hidden nature. All our language will be concerned with what we see, hear, touch or smell, and not with supposed hidden or "'supernatural" realities. Ayer summed this up with what he called the "verification principle" – the meaning of a statement is the method of its verification. To put it another way, if you cannot see or smell something, it makes no sense to talk about it. This is no doubt why Ayer never paid much attention to what other people thought. He couldn't smell their thoughts, so it was meaningless to talk about them. This philosophy got rid of most traditional philosophical questions by showing that they were not just grammatical mistakes; they were actually meaningless.

It follows that both Ryle and Ayer thought that each other's beliefs were mostly meaningless. Ayer was sure that it was nonsense to talk about unverifiable objects (like Ryle's unvoiced thoughts), and Ryle was sure that it was nonsense to talk about "sense-data" (like Ayer's smells). It is not surprising that they could not understand each other. They each thought the other's beliefs were not just mistaken. They were literally nonsensical.

This situation provides a clue to the real nature of philosophy. Philosophers do not deal with particular factual questions, where everybody agrees what a "fact" is, and how to decide whether something is a fact or not (for example, whether light moves in a straight line or not). Philosophers deal with questions about what general scheme of concepts most adequately makes sense of the world. They deal with general conceptual frameworks for understanding and interpreting the world. Anybody who has a different conceptual framework will seem to them to be talking nonsense.

Such frameworks differ considerably from one another. Some think that in the end we should rely on common-sense beliefs and not be led astray by weird theories. Others (sometimes the same people on different days) think that many common-sense beliefs are actually based on linguistic mistakes and that we need a bit of linguistic hygiene to eliminate such mistakes. Some think that, whatever common sense says, we should only trust our sense-perceptions, which tell us how things really exist. Others think that only sense-perceptions really exist and there is nothing else to tell. And yet others, influenced by modern physics, think that we should not rely on either common sense or on sense-perception, since the real world is very much stranger than we think and wholly unrepresentable by the senses.

What is the evidence for the truth of such views? There is nothing that would conclusively settle a dispute between them. However hard Ayer tried to get Ryle to have some sense-data, Ryle would refuse to have them. Not only that, Ryle would deny that there were any such things, even though Ayer was having them all the time. This is clearly not a matter of evidence. It is a matter of which most basic or general concepts we are going to use to interpret our experience. Of course arguments can be presented for and against such basic interpretations, and those arguments seek to show that one favoured view presents an interpretation of the data of human knowledge that is adequate, comprehensive, consistent, fruitful, elegant, and appealing, while all other views are nonsensical – or, it might be more tolerant to say, less adequate interpretations of reality.

My dispute with Ryle, which I probably only have any hope of winning because he is safely dead, is a philosophical debate in this sense. It is not about the ordinary usage of words or about how best to tidy up the informal grammar of our language. It is a dispute about what human persons really are. It is about whether what is of unique importance about human persons is their possession of a rich inner mental life, over which they have some degree of responsible control, and which is quite different in character from and irreducible to the law-governed motions of physical particles in space. It is, to put it in more traditional (though almost universally misunderstood) terms, about whether it is helpful to speak of the human soul as what makes humans of distinctive value and significance.

Ryle and dualism

The Concept of Mind is largely devoted to arguing that the "Cartesian myth" of humans as "ghosts in mechanical machines" is nonsensical, and to proposing a different model of human beings as social animals exhibiting distinctive kinds of intelligent behaviour. The stress is on the primary importance of publicly observable behaviour. But it is not empiricist in the narrow sense that confines all knowledge to immediate data of the senses. Indeed it regards talk of "immediate data of the senses" as artificial and misleading jargon invented by philosophers, when we should just say that sometimes we hear and see things without using telescopes or microscopes.

If Ryle's book convinces, it is not because it provides hitherto unconsidered evidence. It is because it gives a convincing model for understanding human beings as evolved social animals. This fits well with evolutionary biology, with an interest in social psychology and anthropology, and with a general loss of belief in a "soul" which is only possessed by human beings, marking them out as totally different in kind from all other animals. It is also a very non-mechanistic and non-reductionist view, and so makes it possible to retain a form of humanism, stressing the distinctiveness and importance of human capacities and excellences.

Ryle's view, largely shared by Wittgenstein, is proposed as a perspective from which to perceive human nature, and it has been influenced by many converging strands of new factual knowledge, new capabilities, and novel evaluations in rapidly developing social systems. Philosophy changes as previous basic interpretations are felt to be inadequate in some way. It is the fate of each philosophical insight to become the nonsense of its succeeding generation. Descartes celebrated the birth of the new science in the seventeenth century, but Ryle set out to show that the Cartesian philosophy was nonsensical. Perhaps Ryle knew that the same thing was bound to happen to him.

Chapter Nine

In defence of dualism

I begin with the question of whether there are inner experiences to which persons have privileged access and which may not be material objects with spatial location. These would be experiences like sights, sounds, smells and so on (they have been called "sense-data" or "qualia"). Against Ryle, I argue that sensible dualists do not think the mind is a separate hidden world, connected arbitrarily to the body. It is the inner aspect of the material person, but it is a realm of partly unverifiable privately accessed data, and its rich, value-filled complex of feelings, thoughts, and intentions (its "inner life") is a key element of human personhood. Moreover, it is logically possible that this inner aspect could, very unusually, exist without the body. But its proper and normal place is precisely as the inner aspect of a material body and brain, situated in a shared social environment.

Dualism, the original sin of Descartes, is not yet dead. Dualists can be found hiding in the philosophical undergrowth, slightly cowed perhaps but still defiant. The heart of dualism, in the sense relevant to this discussion, is that mind and matter are two distinct sorts of thing. Minds do not exist in space, whereas matter is defined in terms of its location and extent in space. Minds think, feel, and perceive, and matter does not. I have suggested that this is just as much common sense as is Ryle's view, though it is quite possible that common sense may change its mind, if it has one.

It has to be admitted that there is almost a consensus among many modern writers that common sense should give up belief in dualism. Malcolm Jeeves and Warren Brown, both distinguished neuropsychologists who write about the philosophical implications of their work, say, "We believe it is no longer helpful or reasonable to consider mind a nonmaterial entity that can be decoupled from the body." We should no longer consider the "I" to be a separate inner agent, but we must accept that the mind is "a functional property of our brain and body".[1]

I can see what they mean, but I think that what they say is not quite right. In fact, the rest of their excellent book shows just why it is not quite right. It is, to put it bluntly, a bit of undigested anti-Cartesian prejudice. They say that the mind is not a "nonmaterial entity". Yet they also say that consciousness, intelligent thought, and moral decision-making are emergent properties of a complex material system. "The basis of consciousness," they write, "is a dynamically self-organising complex system within the cerebral cortex."[2] But they are careful not to say that consciousness *is* a system in the cerebral cortex and nothing more.

That consciousness is nothing more than physical brain-behaviour they call "reductive physicalism", and they distance themselves from it. They espouse what they call "non-reductive physicalism". Complex systems generate new properties that are not just combinations of properties possessed by the simpler parts of such systems. Nevertheless, they hold that such emergent properties do not introduce any new "stuff" into what the universe is made of. The only stuff out of which things are made is material stuff – fundamental particles or waves or vibrations in a fifth dimension or whatever the favourite basic material stuff may be. (It is not insignificant that physicists are not agreed about what it is. It is not after all totally convincing to be told that everything in existence is definitely made of something, but we are not quite sure just what that something is.)

An example of an emergent property might be the sound of an orchestral chord in a Beethoven symphony, which is an emergent property from the arrangement of fundamental particles which makes up an electromagnetic set of wavelengths. The only physical stuff around is electromagnetic waves at a specific frequency whose physical properties can be specified accurately. Those properties do not include any reference to what a chord sounds like or to its beauty. But when those waves hit the ear and get transmitted to the appropriate area of the brain, hey presto, a beautiful sound appears!

But is the sound of a chord not a kind of stuff? If it exists at all, it is stuff. Could it be just mental stuff? Conscious minds hear specific sound waves as having a specific timbre, pitch, and emotional tone, though none of those properties exist when the sound waves are unheard.

Heard sounds do not appear to be objective physical properties. They are what humans experience sound waves to be, when such waves cause stimulation of the brain. We say that some sounds are beautiful. But what we mean is that we experience them as beautiful. This new property of heard sound, with a pleasing or displeasing character, is not some new behavioural principle that applies to complex arrangements of fundamental particles, whether or not they are being perceived. It is an actual occurrent feeling of something being experienced as emotionally resonant. If that heard sound is not a physical property (one that exists in the absence of conscious beings), then it follows that there must be at least one non-physical property. So this is not a form of "physicalism" at all, either reductive or non-reductive. It has introduced at least one piece of non-physical stuff.

It is true that complex organized physical systems behave in different ways from simple, relatively isolated physical particles. The laws governing the behaviour of such systems cannot be deduced from a study of fundamental particles alone. We could say that the laws of complex organized systems are not reducible to laws governing the behaviour of fundamental particles considered in isolation. Yet that would not license anyone to talk of "new occurrent properties". The properties would remain the same; they would just behave in different ways.

Feelings of wetness, perceptions of colour, and sounds of sonority are occurrences that do not exist in the absence of minds. These are what Ayer used to call "sense-data", though many modern philosophers call them "qualia", and recognize that they are logically distinct from physical properties. They do not just emerge from complex physical systems. They emerge when such complex systems give rise to perceptions. For this reason, Professor John Polkinghorne, from whom I have learned almost all that I know about physics, nevertheless does not seem to me to be quite right when he says, "We can accept a structural reductionism... the units out of which all the entities of the physical world are constructed are just the elementary particles studied by fundamental physics."[3]

He is right when he says that in the physical (unobserved) world there are only elementary particles (or whatever), in various more or less complex arrays. But he is wrong if he means that all that exists is part of the physical world. Perceived sound is not a bit of "meaning" or "information" stuck onto physical particles. It is something we perceive and feel as what the physical world is like when it is apprehended by us.

The obvious conclusion is that perceived properties are caused by physical processes, including brain processes, and those processes must be functioning correctly for us to perceive correctly. But the perceived properties are not out there in the physical objects. They are additional properties caused by complex organized physical systems, and they exist only for and in consciousness.

We assume, most of the time, that effects are different from their causes, and that cause and effect could, logically, exist apart. They could be decoupled. So the "non-reductive physicalists" are really saying that mental properties are caused by physical properties, that when a certain sort of complex organized physical system comes into existence, it causally generates new sorts of conscious stuff. Minds or mental properties emerge from matter. That is a very important thing to say. But it implies that minds are different from matter. They therefore could in principle be decoupled from matter, as any effect could in principle be decoupled from its cause. Causal connections are, after all, contingent. They may hold universally in our universe. But they could have been otherwise. Therefore if the brain–mental state relation is causal, the brain state and the mental state are not strictly identical. Whether Jeeves and Brown like it or not, mental states could in principle be decoupled from brain states, and minds are more than just functional properties of our brains and bodies. We may just have to wait and see.

Do zombies exist?

Some philosophers, who obviously have a liking for horror films, address this point by asking whether there could possibly be zombies. A zombie, for philosophical purposes, is a human body that acts and talks exactly like a human, but has no consciousness, no mental states, at all. It would obviously pass the Turing test – that is, after talking to it for as long as you like, you would still not be able to tell that it was a zombie. You would probably think that it had thoughts and feelings and sensations, just like you. But it might not have.

Is such a thing possible? I have to say that I think it is – and not just because I really suspect that some of the people I meet are zombies. I prefer to give everyone the benefit of the doubt. Yet I can think of borderline cases. For instance, do ants possess consciousness? Do they feel anything or like and dislike things? I tend to think ants operate solely by reacting to chemical stimuli – by stigmergy or programmed behaviour caused by previous behaviour that has changed the immediate environment, and that looks as though it is intelligent (like termites building a rather complicated nest).

If someone built a robot that was more or less indistinguishable from a human being, but the creator knew that his robot consisted just of integrated circuits and programmed routines, she would have good reasons for thinking she had built a zombie. Descartes infamously thought that animals were all zombies. How do we know that they are not? Well, their physiology is very like ours, they have central nervous systems and brains, and their behaviour seems to suggest awareness of pleasure and pain.

A number of experiments by the physiologist Michel Cabanac claim to show that animals and humans both act, at least in laboratory conditions, not to maximize their biological fitness, but to maximize their sensory pleasure. The feeling of pleasure, he holds, is the cause of many behavioural and physiological changes. This suggests that animals are similar to us in being conscious – they feel pleasure. Of course you could still maintain that the feeling is a by-product of the release of chemicals in the brain, which is the real cause of behavioural changes, thereby preserving a materialist view.

There is no experimental way of resolving the issue. It is natural to think that the more like us something is, the more it will share the same sorts of property, including conscious properties. I conclude that zombies are possible, but it is a good thing to extend a personal set of interpretations of and reactions to the world as widely as possible. We take a particular moral stance toward something when we regard it as a conscious agent. Perhaps, as Kant suggested, this is a basic attitude we must adopt to the world if we are to be fully moral agents ourselves, even though it cannot be based on conclusive evidence.

Though we cannot refute Descartes' view of animals, most of us probably now feel that our greatly increased knowledge of the genetic, biological, and psychological properties of animals leads us to adopt a more morally concerned attitude to them. Zombies are possible, but it is a moral failure to assume that they are actual without a very good reason. This shows that moral failures can be failures to interpret the facts, so values and facts are not as distinct as some philosophers have claimed. It also shows that some of our most basic philosophical attitudes are not based on evidence, in the sense of publicly accessible data that can be publicly observed and agreed upon by all competent observers.

There are some widely, though not universally accepted, beliefs that Alvin Plantinga has called "basic beliefs". I will adopt this term for beliefs that are not based on agreed evidence (since we all agree on the available evidence), but for which reasons can be given, reasons that argue for particular beliefs as conditions of a general conceptual scheme that we (some of us) think it right to adopt. They include the belief that people (and animals) are not zombies, that they have an inner consciousness; the belief that the laws of nature will continue to operate, and that there is no event without some sort of cause; the belief that I am a continuing agent of experience and action; that there is mental causality or freedom of action; that I can remember my dreams; that human embryos have a right to life; and, for people like me, the idealist belief that reality is ultimately mind-like.

Common-sense philosophers are right to think that some of our fundamental beliefs are like this. But they do not always see that such beliefs are not all universally agreed, and therefore need not be as common as all that. The reasons given for such beliefs may depend on deep underlying ways of seeing and responding to human experience. But there is no way of gaining universal agreement on such basic ways of seeing and believing. One of these beliefs – the one I am concerned with at present – is that other people are not zombies, but that zombies are possible, and one might in future be constructed in a laboratory.

Seeing faces

Malcolm Jeeves and Warren Brown say they have a rather different basic belief, a belief in the truth of physicalism. They would not like saying that zombies are possible; it entails, after all, a form of dualism, that mental properties are different and decouplable from physical properties. Yet they do say something that strongly implies their possibility. For, they say, their work in neuroscience suggests that subjective experiences often exert a causal influence (a "top-down" influence) on the physical system and its parts.

They stress, for instance, that the cerebral cortex of young humans is plastic or partly unformed and continues to organize and reorganize functional networks of neurons "through experiences, learning, imagination, and thought".[4] They quote Nancy Kanwisher of MIT as saying that "evidence indicates important roles for both genetic factors and specific early experience, in the construction of the Fusiform Face Area". That is, the ability of the adult human to recognize faces depends in part upon the subjective experience of interacting with other people's faces in the first few months of life. Such experience actually modifies the face-perception neurons in the brain to enable them to function more efficiently. Subjective experiences or acts (thoughts) cause changes in the physical structure of the brain. Emergent mental properties and experiences "have a real influence on behaviour".[5] How, then, can they continue to say that "humans are taken to be entirely physical"?

Perhaps they mean that humans are physical entities that possess nonmaterial properties, but that there are no nonmaterial *entities*. Unfortunately, that would require a clear distinction between entities and properties that would be very hard to defend. Properties just are entities that coexist with or depend upon other sets of properties.

They could still say that nonmaterial properties (like conscious experiences) could not exist without the brain properties which are their basis. But what is the force of such a "could not"? We might say that there is a strong causal connection between them – though, as I have noted, this causality runs both ways, from brain states to subjective experiences and from thoughts to neuronal connections in the brain. Where there is a causal connection in fact, there need not have been or there could have been a different one. We could have brains without consciousness or consciousness without brains. Those who believe there is a God who knows what is going on in the world actually believe that there is a consciousness without a brain – God is conscious, but has no brain. Admittedly God is very different from human minds, but the point is that many people at least think they can conceive of a consciousness without a body. If they are right, we cannot rule out the possibility of a human consciousness existing without its normal body by saying that such a thing is inconceivable.

The world would be decidedly odd if causal connections between brains and experiences kept breaking down. This is another basic, unevidenced attitude we take to the world – we trust that causal laws will not break down for no reason. Nevertheless, in extreme situations, like the death of the body for example, such connections may well break down. We cannot refute the hypothesis of continued consciousness after death, without a brain, just by saying it is impossible. Philosophers sometimes do say that, admittedly. But even philosophers should not deny possibilities *a priori*, just because they seem peculiar to them.

The embodied mind

I conclude that minds, subjects of experiences and intentional acts, are after all nonmaterial and can be decoupled from specific brains. Moreover, that is entailed by any genuinely non-reductive physicalism, which is not, when analysed more closely, really physicalism (materialism) at all. Yet what Jeeves and Brown are saying is important. Minds need an environment to provide experiential data, and also to provide an arena in which to perform actions and to interact with other minds. Our physical world is not the only possible form of environment for minds. There may be other universes different from ours, with different kinds of minds in them. But human minds need to be genuinely embodied and embedded in some sort of environment. Minds are directed upon a world of objects, both by attention and by intention. Our minds may be causally limited to this physical world and they have certainly emerged within it by a long process of evolutionary development. They are not self-contained and only externally related to the physical world.

We can thus say that minds read or interpret the configuration of neurons which store information that the brain has received from its environment. They may then influence this configuration by thought and further experience. The configuration is stored in the brain (as a symphony is stored on a CD) and is ready to be read again (remembered) at a later time.

This way of putting the matter requires that the brain functions properly. Configurations and interpretations can go wrong, and if the physical basis is blocked or damaged, they will go wrong. So it is not at all surprising that brain damage will cause predictable mental defects or that particular mental processes are often found to be localized in specific areas of the brain. Such facts are to be expected by sensible dualists, who of course believe that minds think about objects in the world and try to perform actions in the world, and have never believed that minds only contemplate special mental objects and perform special mental actions in a special mental world. There are mental objects (like images) and there are mental actions (like thoughts). But these are derivative from the physical objects toward which minds are naturally and properly directed. That is just what poor maligned Descartes actually thought.

What is important about dualism is that it retains belief in the moral primacy of personal experience and morally responsible action. But it does not deny that human experience is primarily of a physical world and that free acts are performed in a physical and public world.

Living in two worlds

It is possible that our subjective mental life may not in fact be separable from the activity of our bodies. I think that is a matter that argument alone cannot resolve. It may be that the interweaving of mind and body is so close and complex that it would not make sense, if we fully analysed it, to speak of a mental life anything like ours continuing without the very same physical world in which it has developed and lived. Then what Jeeves and Brown say would be correct. But I do not think we can be sure of this, and I think it is wiser to remain open to the possibility of a continuation of mental life after bodily death.

In dreams we experience the possibility of conscious knowledge and action which does not take place in an actual physical world. Admittedly dream images seem to be constructed from past experiences of a physical world. But it is fairly easy to conceive of images that occur in the mind without any physical cause and which might be shared between different minds. We can conceive of image-worlds that some groups of minds share, but which do not form the sort of objective causal nexus that exists in our physical universe.

The philosopher H. H. Price has sketched such an image-world in his little book, *Lectures in the Philosophy of Religion*. In his image-world, persons meet in rather flexible image-bodies (rather like avatars in a video game) insofar as they are psychically attracted to one another, and the causal laws are such that desires directly cause desired "physical" states to exist. This may sound very attractive, until we realize that always getting what we want may turn out to be a disadvantage, as King Midas could tell us. And also the people we would be psychically attracted to might turn out to be as horrible as we are, which could be very uncomfortable. Indeed, it might be a sort of hell.

Another idea of an image-world is presented by the Oxford philosopher Anthony Quinton, who sketches the slightly alarming possibility that every night when we go to sleep, we may have such coherent dreams that we actually seem to live in a quite different world. After a hard night's work in the other world, we go to sleep, and immediately dream of being back in this world. That seems a coherent idea, though it also threatens to be a very tiring one. When, if ever, would we get a good night's sleep? Anyway, if this happened which would be the real world? I suppose they would both be equally real, and we would be the same person, not just in two different bodies, but in two different worlds.

Such possibilities require some mechanism by which images could be generated or by which minds could continue to exist with new forms of experience and capacities for intentional action. In the absence of such a mechanism, it will probably be true that even if minds are immaterial (or contain important sets of non-physical properties), they will not in fact be separable from the bodies and brains that form their physical substrata.

There may, however, be various mechanisms that could ensure the decoupling of minds from bodies. The most obvious one is a supreme cosmic mind of some sort that could arrange for appropriate experiences to occur to "decoupled minds", perhaps as moral consequences of what they have done in their physical bodies. Or, as in some Buddhist philosophies, there could be an impersonal moral law (**karma**) which brings into existence image-worlds (detailed in *The Tibetan Book of the Dead*, for example) in which the moral consequences of human life-choices can be worked out. Yet another possibility is that, if there are many alternative universes which have sprung from the primal quantum vacuum, we might not need to travel through a black hole to get into another universe. We may just have to go to sleep – a very economical form of travel.

The philosopher Professor Ayer, one of the most vociferous philosophical atheists of his day, was extremely surprised to find that he continued to have experiences after he had died. He came back to life after being clinically dead, and his experiences, though they were odd in the extreme, were momentous enough for him to accept the possibility of life after death. This he found very disappointing personally, as it conflicted with most of his previous philosophy. Yet for anyone who is not a materialist, some kind of existence after death remains a possibility, disappointing or not.

That possibility requires that either dualism or idealism is true. So I do not think we should give up the idea that there is an immaterial self, in the sense outlined in chapter five, a subject of experience and action that is not bound to the conditions of this earthly body and that could be decoupled from this body and brain. But we should certainly accept the overwhelming evidence from neurological research that our minds are emergent realities from physical processes and are strongly embedded in physical environments through brain, body, and networks of social-historical relationships. Such evidence is quite compatible with sophisticated forms of both dualism and idealism, and it even points to the need for a more holistic view of minds as embedded in networks of social relationships, rather than as isolated units confined to individual skulls. That is where the work of Ryle and Wittgenstein provides a healthy antidote to materialism.

In this chapter I have argued that there is a real question of whether minds and contents of consciousness are special kinds of entities ("stuff") that are not reducible to material properties. This is not a pseudo-problem or one that could be resolved simply by appeal to how we ordinarily use words. Yet it is also not a question that can be resolved by appeal to evidence, in the sense of publicly accessible and decisively verifiable data. It is more a question of interpreting the data we have in the most adequate way – and what is most adequate is itself not universally agreed or conclusively decidable.

I suggested that it is partly a moral stance to adopt the basic belief that other persons are genuine moral agents, not zombies. But the existence of qualia or "private" experiences, and the seeming existence of "top-down" causation in neuropsychology can lead to adopting the belief that minds are more than brains. It seems to follow that the mind–brain connection is causal and contingent, and that minds could logically exist without brains. However, this may be only a bare logical possibility, and it certainly seems that human minds emerge from and are closely integrated with brain-events. It is not essential to Cartesian dualism that minds actually do exist in a disembodied state. What matters is that, even if human minds are essentially embodied, what is morally important about human persons depends upon their uniquely appropriated experiences and responsibly free actions; that is, upon distinctively mental properties.

Chapter Ten

Consciousness, value, and purpose

A crucial question is whether human persons are morally free and responsible. This is a question which there seems to be no possibility of resolving empirically, yet to which arguments, like the ones discussed in this book, are relevant, and which it is important to decide in practice. The psychologist Benjamin Libet has tried to put the issue to experimental test, but the tests do not really seem to touch on the issue of moral freedom, and they do not appear to resolve the issue. I accept Immanuel Kant's view that we need to decide the issue on practical grounds – it is morally important to treat persons as free and responsible, even if we cannot theoretically prove they are.

In addition, we experience ourselves as envisaging possible futures, evaluating them, and choosing between them. It is reasonable to take these experiences as telling us what is true of reality – we really are free and able to cause physical changes by thought and intention. No relatively abstract theory should cause us to renounce these deliverances of experience.

The real threat to Ryle has not been a revival of dualism. It has been the rise of materialism. The development of neuroscience and of artificial intelligence has suggested to some philosophers that consciousness is not as important as we used to think. Computers can be built to perform intelligent operations. They (or at least one of them) can even beat the best human chess-players in the world, and they can think millions of times more quickly than humans. But they do not need to be conscious.

Studies of the brain have shown that humans do not need to be conscious either. Experiments with patients with brain damage have shown that they can tell the location or movements of objects in their vicinity with an accuracy well above average even when they are not aware of any visual stimuli – that is, when they cannot see them. This remarkable phenomenon, known as blindsight, seems to show that the brain can respond to stimuli without being conscious of them. Some experiments seem to show that the brain can "make decisions" before any conscious decision has been made. These experiments have been hailed by materialists as showing that awareness and free will are by-products of physical brain processes, and that the belief that I can make decisions freely is an illusion.

The best-known experiments in this respect are those by Benjamin Libet. In his most famous experiment, he put human subjects in a laboratory, attached EEG electrodes to their skulls to measure electrical activity in their brains, and attached an electromyograph (EMG) to their arm muscles. He then asked them to press a button at any time selected by them within a short period of time. The EEG measured when a particular sort of cortical activity occurred (called the "readiness potential", which generally occurs as pre-motor planning of volitional movements). The EMG reading measured when the button was actually pressed. And the subjects were asked to note the moment (as measured by a dot moving around a huge clock) when they made the decision to press the button.

The results, confirmed over many experiments, were that the readiness potential occurred in the brain about 300 milliseconds before the stated decision to act, which in turn occurred about 200 milliseconds before the button was actually pressed. Libet's conclusion was that the brain initiates movement, and the apparently "free" decision comes after movement has been initiated. So it seems all causation happened at the unconscious level of the brain, and the conscious decision to act played no part in the proceedings at all. Free will has been disproved!

If this were true, it would be very worrying indeed for anyone, like an idealist, who thinks that the mind can initiate actions in a non-physical way, and that such decisions have physical effects. It seems to show that all real causes are physical, and that the sense of "acting freely" is totally superfluous and, in fact, illusory.

As we might expect, however, this sort of experiment is very controversial, and what it really shows is not very clear. One major consideration is the very artificial situation of the person being asked to press the button. When we are interested in free decision-making, we are mostly concerned with important moral decisions, when someone has to choose between right and wrong and can be held responsible for their choice. Or we might be concerned with the nature of creative choices in painting or music or with reasoning activities in mathematics or philosophy. These are real-life issues where we want to know if mental states can make a causal difference, which might have been otherwise, to what happens in the physical world.

All such factors are missing in the Libet experiments. The subject is asked to press a button at a completely arbitrary time, and say when he or she was "aware of the urge to act". In fact, the primary intention has been completed before the experiment begins. That intention is to execute a slight and pointless physical movement at some arbitrary time in the near future. There is no moral or rational or artistic significance in the action; it really does not matter when or how often it takes place.

Since we know that a great many bodily actions – like breathing or eating – are virtually automatic, it is hardly surprising that the mind (whose job it is to find reasons for acting) hands over the task of pressing a button to the automatic brain, because there is no reason for choosing one time over any other time. The intention is to press the button at an arbitrary time. There is no reason to press it or not press it at any particular time. The brain has been instructed to do that, so it does.

When the conscious mind "becomes aware of the urge to act", which has been arbitrarily selected by the unconscious motor system of the brain, there is no reason to suppress that urge. The mind assents and records the time at which it does so. It may seem as if the mind is merely following the dictates of electrical activity in the brain. But the fact is that the mind had already agreed to do precisely that when it formed the intention to take part in the experiment and to press the button arbitrarily (that is, for no reason). The only point at which a significantly free decision was made was at the point of deciding to participate in the experiment. So all the experiment shows is that some fairly arbitrary "decisions to act" are parts of behavioural routines that proceed automatically, but which may themselves be initiated by real mental decisions.

Libet himself was a believer in freedom of the will, and argued that the mind could always veto the "urge to act" if it had reason to do so. But my point is rather wider than that. It is that experimental situations are very special. They abstract from real-life situations, and introduce artificial factors like "moving a finger for no reason" to substitute for really significant factors like "deciding whether to kill someone for personal gain". Naturally we do not want to construct experiments that will put such real-life questions to the test. But that means the results of the experiments we can do, fascinating though they are, do not address the problem of human freedom in any really illuminating way.

Experimental tests on human persons mimic real-life situations in a distorted and artificially restricted way. They do not show what "really happens" in real-life situations. They show how some abstracted aspects of real-life situations can be mimicked in a laboratory. Much useful information about the brain can be obtained from such experiments. But it should not be thought that laboratory results show us what really happens in real life, where a huge variety of complex, interconnected, and unmeasurable factors contribute to our conscious experience of acting and intending to act.

Is consciousness useless?

There is good reason to think that conscious states are real and causally efficacious, but it could be argued that consciousness is a disadvantage, an evolutionary mistake. If we were not conscious, we would not feel pain, we would not get depressed, and we would not waste time by asking silly questions like "Why am I here?" or "What's it all about?" Consciousness helps animals to see and try to escape their predators. But it would be more efficient to have an automatic stimulus-response-escape mechanism. Possibly ants have. They hardly have big enough brains to be conscious, yet they manage to fight, reproduce, and communicate very well. So we might have survived very well as communities of unfeeling robots. Information could have been processed, long molecules of DNA could have reproduced, and vast banks of knowledge could have been built up – but no one would have understood such knowledge or would even have been aware of it. It would just have been there, coded in complex systems of condensed algorithms. It would have been a universe in which CD-ROMs of amazing complexity would have been assembled, encapsulating every possible word and melody and thought that ever could exist, but without those thoughts and notes ever actually occurring to any consciousness. All the great literature of the world would have existed, but would never have been read or understood.

If you ask, "What would be the point of that?", the point is that there is not, and never has been, any point. It just is. Of course there may be no point in the existence of consciousness either. But the existence of consciousness introduces evaluation into the discussion. There may be no ultimate point in anything, but some things are more pointless than others. Counting the number of hairs on my legs is more pointless than trying to alleviate a headache. Since consciousness involves pleasure and pain, there is always a point in ending pain and obtaining pleasure.

Pleasure can be pointless, too, but it is always preferable to pain – unless the pain is a warning of greater pain to come. The greatest pleasures, according to philosophers as diverse as Aristotle and John Stuart Mill, are those which engage the human faculties in active and creative ways. People are happiest when they do things they are good at and interested in, with a reasonable degree of success, and when others appreciate what they are doing. Consciousness is essentially bound up with intentional action, because conscious beings seek to avoid pain and pursue pleasure. The very complex physical structures of the brain that make awareness possible also enable intentions to guide the physical movements of the body.

Computers do not feel pain or seek to avoid it. They are designed (programmed) by humans to do specific tasks, information is inputted by humans, and outputted information is then interpreted by humans. Computers, like telescopes, are instruments designed to enable conscious beings to achieve new knowledge and to modify the world in new ways. Computers are tools and take no pleasure in winning chess games. They will win if they are programmed well, and if they are instructed to, and that is it. Computers are very bad models for human beings, as they lack awareness, evaluation, and purpose, the very qualities that are distinctively personal.

This is the enormous difference that consciousness makes. Consciousness may not be necessary for complex organisms to develop, but it does introduce a new element to reality, the element of understanding and appreciating a state of affairs. This element is quite different from any purely physical state, and it cannot be reduced to or described in terms of any purely physical state. It also introduces a new purposive form of causality, based on the envisaging and evaluation of future conscious states and activities. In having a purpose, minds have to envisage a possible state as a future state. This representation of something *as future* is a distinctively mental property. The occurrent state, which of course exists now in some mind, represents a state that does not yet exist. Knowing that some state is about the future, or even about the non-existent, is not itself a physical property. It is the "aboutness" that makes the difference. It is what has been called an **"intensional state"**, a state that symbolizes something other than its own physical properties.

The evaluation of a possible future as good or bad, desirable or undesirable, is similarly a mental property. Machines can be programmed to reach specific physical states and then stop. But there is no sense in saying that they think about such states and are pleased when they reach them. "Goodness" is not a physical property of anything. To say that something is good is to say that it is the object of rational choice, choice directed by the thought that something would be pleasant or otherwise desirable. There is no place in any physical science for such concepts.

The formation of an intention to do something in future is also not a physical property, as it signifies that a future state will be brought about by intelligent action. The idea of final causality, of acting in order to obtain a desired future, as a cause of action through ideas, is a distinctively mental idea of causality. Bacon was right; there are no final causes in a purely material world.

The natural sciences presuppose the basic postulate that there are measurable and intelligible law-like regularities in nature. This postulate is confirmed by experience and is the basis of scientific explanation and prediction. In a similar way the experiences of practical reasoning, creative imagination, and moral commitment presuppose the basic postulate that there exists free and reason-based action. This postulate too is confirmed by experience and is the basis of personal relationship and understanding. Any adequate account of our world must include both postulates in a coherently related framework.

The idea of purely physical causality is a very sophisticated concept that remains almost wholly mysterious in nature. It could be said that our primary sense of causality, the one that we most directly and commonly experience, is that of bringing something about for the sake of a desired goal. Personal causality is something we experience and have to assume if we are to live as persons. Physical causality is, by comparison, a stripped-down abstract idea of regular law-like connections between physical events considered in artificially isolated conditions. In physical causality, one thing follows another, but nothing is actually brought about by any active power, and there are no goals set by any being. It seems strange, then, that anyone should think that personal causality may be an illusion, whereas only physical causality is objectively real. Such a counter-intuitive belief can only be accounted for by a strong prior commitment to a strictly materialist point of view that ignores the all-pervading evidence of personal experience.

We can make a meaningful distinction between behaviour that blindly executes a routine without any goal being actually envisaged, and conscious pursuit of an envisaged goal. Even those who think that the idea of intelligent design in nature is an illusion have to know what an intelligent, purposive action would be or they would not be able to say what it is that does not actually exist. Once that possibility is allowed, it is a matter of experience to determine whether it is actual. It is our own experience that we envisage, evaluate, and intend, and it would take an overwhelmingly strong theory to overturn that experience. I do not believe there is any such theory.

Why consciousness is essential

It is only with consciousness that the concepts of value and purpose, which are central to our social life, to living as persons among other persons, make sense. I doubt if these concepts make any sense for a ruthlessly materialist view of reality. They would, it may be said, be purely subjective. But even in that case purely subjective realities would exist, and that is just what a materialist denies.

The philosopher G. E. Moore asked people to envisage a very beautiful and elegant universe that was not consciously perceived by any being and to compare it with a very ugly and chaotic universe, similarly unperceived. He thought the beautiful universe was obviously better. But only philosophers can seriously claim that objects that no one has ever seen or will ever see are beautiful. It is rather like saying that ice cream that has never been eaten tastes wonderful. It might taste wonderful if someone ate it. Otherwise it has no taste at all. Most of us know that conscious experience adds properties – like beauty and pleasure – to the universe that otherwise would never exist at all.

I have discussed the fact that many philosophers, beginning with Galileo, make a sharp distinction between "secondary qualities" like colour, taste, smell, pleasure, and pain, that only exist in consciousness, and "primary qualities" like mass, position, and momentum, that exist in non-conscious reality. Yet such primary qualities in turn seem to dissolve into spatially located or extended fields of force or even into the completely "veiled reality" that Kant and d'Espagnat postulate.

This is a long way from materialism, which claims that primary qualities are pretty well known and are the only constituent elements of reality. For some quantum physicists, like Niels Bohr, one of the fathers of quantum physics, the primary qualities of the physical world are almost wholly mysterious and seem more like mathematical abstractions from the directly experienced world of colours, sounds, smells – and of beauty, elegance, pleasure, and pain.

It may well seem that the "real" world is the experienced world, the world that exists in conscious experience. This is the view taken by idealist philosophers, who completely reverse the materialist hypothesis. For materialism, the emergence of awareness, evaluation, and purpose from unconscious, unfeeling, and purposeless physical processes is a puzzle, and a pretty pointless one at that.

Idealists hypothesize that fundamental reality includes awareness, evaluation, and purpose – that mind is more basic, more causally efficacious, than matter. For an idealist, the existence of a material world is not such a great puzzle, because finite minds need physical expression if they are to relate to one another; if they are to have objects of knowledge that can please or displease them; and if they are to have goals that they can try to achieve in a partly pliable but partly resistant environment. Moreover, minds give an additional sort of explanation for why physical laws exist as they do – namely, they exist in order to allow a wide variety of worthwhile states to be realized and appreciated.

Most idealists think that since the universe existed long before any finite minds came to exist within it, there is something mind-like at the basis of the physical universe itself. There is a cosmic awareness that envisages all possible states, ranks them evaluatively, and has the purpose of realizing its nature by generating societies of minds in an emergent universe – minds of many grades of awareness and intelligence, which can act in many creative ways to generate new forms of awareness, of beauty and intelligibility. This cosmic awareness is often called God, at least by philosophers.

It sounds a little too personal or anthropomorphic to some idealists, and they prefer to speak in a more Platonic way of an eternal realm of possibilities, beyond even mind or consciousness as we understand it, which necessarily realizes itself through the emergence of conscious and purposive beings, by processes of complex integration between simpler spatio-temporal elements. This is generally known in the German and early twentieth-century British idealist tradition as "the Absolute", and in the Indian *Advaita* tradition as *Brahman*. Consciousness as we know it then is emergent rather than primordial, but it is still an irreducible and causally efficacious element of reality, and it is the inherent goal or purpose of the cosmic process.

That seems to me the most satisfactory picture of the cosmos that can be obtained both from philosophy and from modern science. It may seem that Ryle would disagree completely with this picture, as he seems to deny that inner private conscious events exist at all. But it is not quite so simple. A different, more sympathetic way of interpreting Ryle is that he is saying (and this is even more so in the case of Wittgenstein) that inner conscious events need to have public and physical expressions, and could not exist as they do without being parts of networks of social relationships. Persons are only persons in community, not in isolation. That is why we might want a "dual-aspect" view rather than an outright dualist one.

The inner reality exists, but it could not exist fully and properly as it does without the outer expression. Materialism and idealism both err if they deny any existence to mind or to matter. Both must go together, but for an idealist the driving force of the whole process is in the end the mind-like, the conscious and intentional, with its values and purposes. It is to that existence that the material cosmos points, and in which it finds the fulfilment of its inherent potentialities.

Chapter Eleven

Thoughts and perceptions

Thoughts are an integral part of human consciousness.
Without thoughts we would be unable to interpret
or reflect upon our sense-experiences. Of course we
learn the language in which we usually think from
others. But what we think, the way in which we
think, and the specific content of our thoughts, is
often hidden from others. This does not mean, as
Ryle says, that our thoughts take place in a hidden
parallel universe that can never be discovered at all.
It means that there are important elements of our
inner lives that remain unique to us and that build
up, if we are fortunate, an integrated and structured
perspective on the world that imparts to our lives a
unique value and significance. It is our inner lives of
thoughts and feelings that make us what we are.

For Ryle, who thinks that the Cartesian myth of substantial minds imagines ghosts hiding inside bodily machines, idealists sound as if they are saying that there is a huge super-ghost (a cosmic substantial mind) in the cosmic machine or perhaps that lots of ghosts flit around its more complicated parts. In one sense Ryle is right. There is no cosmic machine and there are no ghosts hiding in its works. Idealists think that the universe includes an important dimension of awareness and purpose or perhaps many sorts of awareness and many diverse purposes. Perhaps these are present as real potentialities in a realm beyond space-time, and space-time is the expressive medium in which they develop to their fullest realization. This might very well suit Ryle's vision of humans as neither angels nor machines, but as intelligent beings whose behaviour expresses their natures in social and creative interaction.

Yet Ryle is also importantly wrong. There are few real dualists who have believed in ghosts. They do not usually believe that there are two completely parallel worlds, one visible and one invisible. What Ryle attacks are often straw men, or straw ghosts, after all. His own language discloses that he is, paradoxically, nearer to the Descartes of reality, not of myth, than he suspects.

Consider what Ryle says about the intellect, in chapter two of *The Concept of Mind*. He opposes the claim that if we speak of an "intelligent" action we are referring to occult episodes in which intelligent minds contemplate a set of true propositions. On such a view, intelligent overt acts are the effects of such unobservable acts of inner contemplation. Ryle wishes to maintain that assertions about intelligent action are explanatory-cum-predictive assertions that can be publicly observed and tested.

By an occult episode he means some invisible action, like assenting to a theoretical truth, which is complete in itself, but which then contingently happens to cause some physical movement of the body. So we could give a complete account of occult actions without mentioning the body at all. It is an almost accidental truth that I think, "If I move my arm I will catch this ball. I want to catch the ball, so I will need to move my arm," and then my arm moves. Ryle believes that on such an account, the intellectual act and the physical act just coincide – though if we are not well coordinated they may not coincide very often. Every physical act is preceded by an invisible piece of syllogistic reasoning, and the link between that reasoning and my bodily movements is wholly mysterious. Life is a perpetual surprise, as my thoughts are often followed by bodily movements, though I have no idea how or why. Most actions also take rather a long time, as I have to go through a series of internal arguments before I do anything. Dualists of this kind are likely to be very slow-moving creatures, who will probably be eaten before they have gone through the arguments in favour of running away.

Does anyone seriously think this, however? Humans are organisms, constantly receiving stimuli from their environment and actively responding to them. Catching a ball is usually pretty automatic and takes no thought at all. But I can pay attention to my technique and improve it through practice. Is that "paying attention" an occult episode? Of course calling it occult is meant to make it seem weird. The occult is the secret and slightly crazy. And my paying attention is not occult in the sense of being completely unknowable by anyone else. I know when you are paying attention. You stare fixedly, you do not just look out of the window, your body is tensed. That is because attending is not a purely private act. It guides bodily processes, modifying their natural responses by targeted mental effort. The mind directly affects the body, to increase the amount and quality of information the senses provide.

Nevertheless, attending is not just bodily behaviour. If attending "consisted in" the presence of testable predictive assertions about behaviour, then it would not matter if I was conscious or not. Yet, as Ryle says, "There are some things which I can find out about you only... through being told of them by you."[1] They include facts about exactly what you see when you attend, what it looks like, and how clearly you see it.

So Ryle amends the account that attending *consists in* specific sorts of bodily behaviour, and retreats to saying that attending is normally *expressed in* bodily behaviour. But he holds that our private internal imaginings are only a small part of human lives, and that only for the mentally ill do they play more than a very minor role. If that is so, there are many more mentally ill people around than Ryle supposed. The richness, complexity, and variety of what I see when

I attend is known to me, but cannot be conveyed with any adequacy either in words or in behaviour. Poets and novelists are better at it than philosophers, and they are the first to say that no words can capture the sheer exuberant profusion of sensory experience.

We can observe people attending, but we cannot observe what they see when they attend. Similarly, we observe people intending, exerting efforts, and trying to perfect their actions. But we cannot observe just how much their efforts contribute to their behaviour, how difficult it is for them or what degree of freedom they have to modify their actions by strength of will.

Persons have hidden lives, which others know nothing about and could never learn from their behaviour, which is often ambiguous or even dissimulative. Where Ryle is right is in seeing that the hidden is capable of being disclosed, and that it is essential that it should normally be disclosed. Our mental acts do not take place in a different parallel world. They take place in this shared and physical world, as experiences of it and actions within it. The unspoken thought and the uttered word are two aspects of the same reality, and though they may exist apart, it is natural for them to exist together, and for each aspect to be modified by the other. I learn a language from others, but I can then modify the way language is used by my own creative deployment of words. This, I think, is what Descartes actually thought, though it seems that his thoughts did not get expressed in words that conveyed his thoughts clearly enough for some other philosophers.

Thinking of coffee

The statement that I am now thinking about a cup of coffee is, despite Ryle's denials, an untestable categorical proposition, and is not just an improbably large set of testable, hypothetical "if-then" statements about how I am liable to behave in proximity to coffee cups. No one can know whether I am lying about my thought or not. You have to take my word for it. It is a prime example of a factual claim that is not capable of public verification.

I could say, as Ayer did, that I can privately verify it. But is that really so? After all, my thought passes very quickly, and my memory is very bad. By the time I get round to verifying whether I am thinking about coffee, I have stopped thinking about it, and instead I am thinking about verification. So I have to depend on memory, and I have no way of checking that my memory is correct. The truth is that I cannot even conclusively verify my own experiences. I can only say that it seems to me that I had them. I am certainly the best judge of whether or not I did have them, but I am not wholly reliable. There is no reason why introspection should be infallible, but that does not mean introspection does not exist. I just have to put up with saying that it seems to me that I thought about coffee – and if I did not believe myself most of the time, I would be in deep trouble.

Maybe we have to drop the verification principle, in the sense of proving the truth of a statement by being confronted with an undeniable sense-experience. We could replace it with something like a fiduciary principle. I have some thoughts or perceptions, and I just have to trust that I have identified them and remember them correctly.

The amazing thing about natural science is that many people have very similar perceptions, and they can produce descriptions that predict some future perceptions pretty well, because perceptions happen to recur in regular ways and in partly controllable conditions. But when we come to our own thoughts, some of us have highly unusual ones. They are not widely shared by others, they do not occur in accordance with some general law, and they do not recur in experimentally controlled conditions.

Consider Einstein thinking of the theory of relativity. This was a totally new and unique thought at the time. There is no law that will make it occur to people in regular ways. And there is little you can do to make it occur to others at all. You can teach them of course but that is conveying the thought to them, not causing it to occur in their brains by creating the right conditions. Nobody doubts that Einstein thought of the theory of relativity.

Yet nobody, not even Einstein himself, can verify that he did. All we can do is to claim that he was the person who first wrote it down, and trust all those who have told us that, and that they got it right.

So there are millions of facts the occurrence of which is not strictly verifiable, either privately or publicly. They include all factual claims about our own thoughts, perceptions, and feelings. We just make a claim on the basis of personal experience and trust that we are probably right. If our behaviour conflicts with such a claim – if, for instance, we say that we hate smoking, while at the same time inhaling a cigar – we have a problem. But it is not obvious that the behaviour should always overrule our personal report. We may indeed hate smoking, but have decided, just once, to be bloody-minded and do something completely unreasonable, just to show that life is absurd. Thoughts and perceptions are different from and not reducible to behaviour.

In a similar way, my thoughts and perceptions are normally, and perhaps always, accompanied by or "expressed in" electrochemical activity in my brain. Yet no amount of electrical or chemical terminology will tell anyone the contents of my thoughts. It may be possible to say what kind of experience I am having when a particular part of my brain displays enhanced blood-flow or electrical activity. I can tell whether it is a visual experience or an aural experience, for example. But to find this out I have to ask the brain's owner what sort of experience is occurring, and then assume that similar brain-events will correlate with similar experiences in future. I may be able to tell that Einstein is thinking in abstract mathematical terms about space-time. But I will not be able to state the theory of relativity just by inspecting Einstein's brain.

Einstein's brain

Einstein's brain was for many years kept in a jar by Dr Harvey of Princeton Hospital, perhaps in the hope that it might one day be stimulated to produce a new and revolutionary physical theory. But if it did, how would we understand it? If we had a neurological dictionary correlating each brain-event with some word or letter, we could write down all the words the brain uttered, like reading a morse-code message. As long as the brain spoke English (or some other known language), we would understand Einstein's brain.

This assumes that there is a one-to-one correlation between phonemes and identifiable and discrete brain states (which is not at all obvious and almost certainly not the case), and that thoughts are always formulated in some grammatically correct language (which is even less obvious). Still, it may be possible to "read thoughts", as long as people are happy to stay connected to brain scanners while they are thinking. That would not be very different from telepathy, an alleged direct knowledge of what someone else is thinking. It would certainly not show that thoughts and brain states were identical. We would just have to assume that each brain state correlated with a specific thought or part of a thought. Whether or not this is so is a factual question, the answer to which cannot be decided by a mere verbal definition. Yet we could never check that or verify it. The best we could do would be to use the fiduciary principle and believe what the brain said when we asked it.

I suspect it would say, "Get me out of here!" or "Leave my brain alone." There might be problems in getting it to concentrate on problems in physics, if it realized its rather unusual situation. But the stubborn fact is that while we can observe neurons firing in the brain, we cannot observe what the brain is conscious of when its neurons are firing.

There is an additional problem. Presumably brains function in accordance with the laws of physics. But Einstein's brain also functions in accordance with the laws of logic and of mathematical deduction. Could we, just using the laws of physics, predict what Einstein's brain would say next? Or would we need to know how to do differential equations before we could say what state his brain would be in when he had finished solving such an equation?

Computers, functioning entirely in accordance with the laws of physics, can solve differential equations – but only if the rules of deduction have been put into them by intelligent minds. Physical pathways can be constructed to produce results in accordance with stateable rules, of logic or of anything else, such as chess. But computers will not know that they have reached a result. They simply follow the rules and then stop, without any idea of what they were trying to do, and without any knowledge that they have solved anything.

This shows that "trying to achieve a goal" and "succeeding" are not ideas that occur in physics, though they can be expressed in purely physical events, if those events are organized in a specific way.

A Brahms symphony can be fully expressed in the physical structure of a compact disc. But a recital of the string of binary digits that make up the compact disc would not sound as attractive as hearing the symphony. Brahms was not trying to write strings of binary digits. He was trying to write beautiful music. That could be put into binary strings, but then some device is needed (a CD-player) to turn those strings back into sounds, which can be heard as violin, not just binary, strings.

If I suggest that the binary strings just organize themselves without even having any conception of what music is, and by chance they happen to play a Brahms symphony, it would be hard to take me seriously. It is the same with the brain. People do not try to make various sets of neurons fire. Most people do not even know what neurons are exactly, much less how to start firing them. Someone may try to solve an equation. The mental acts they perform in the course of doing this can be translated into physical brain states, but it is the purposefully directed acts that decide the order in which brain states occur. They do not just put themselves into a certain order, which miraculously makes me argue in a correct deductive way. The brain states then have to be translated back into mathematical symbols, understood by a human mind to be an argument with premises and a conclusion.

On this account, the brain is a highly organized mechanism for performing mathematical operations, for storing them, and for translating them into occurrent thoughts – axioms, operations, and conclusions. The brain's operations are all purely physical, but its structure, the ordering of its successive states in a logical argument, and the understanding that what has gone on is an argument, and not just a succession of physical states, are all non-physical.

The brain from the inside

Ryle insists that it would be a mistake to think that there is some inner replica of the brain which structures the brain, and which orders and understands its physical states. He is right; the mind is not an inner replica of the brain. It does not repeat what the brain does on an invisible inner stage. Yet the brain has an inner aspect. Not only does it appear to others as an electrochemically active lump of porridge, but it also is known to itself as a set of thoughts, feelings, and intentions.

The structure of the brain has evolved from simpler stimulus-response structures, as organisms come to have more complex and sensitive responses to their environment. Rocks do not have a rich and vibrant inner life. They do not even have the complex organization that would make such a life possible. It is not until central nervous systems develop that anything like consciousness appears in some sort of feeling-life, the nature of which we can hardly imagine. Intelligent consciousness is the inner aspect of the complex organized physical systems we call brains.

At that stage, the organization itself becomes a new phenomenal and causal factor in the behaviour of organisms. At simple inorganic levels the laws of nature are fairly simple, routine, and repetitive in their operation. The laws of mechanics are almost sufficient to describe what is going on. But at complex organic levels new laws come into operation which are more subtle, and exhibit novelty and creativity. The inner life of organisms is not captured by simple physical laws – that is the mistake of reductionism. More complex laws of psychology, of social relationship, and of personal creativity, must be added to the simpler physical bases of behaviour in order to understand human life. Some behaviour will not fall under general laws at all, because of its unique complexity.

We need not think of mind as a complete substantial entity, which mirrors the activity of the brain or body. We can think of it as developing various degrees of awareness and creative responsiveness, as the inner aspect of what appears to us as the physical organism. We might say that there are two modes of access to the same reality, which is active and emergent. There is no threat to this view in saying that all mental operations are strongly correlated with brain processes. But we might want to stress the importance of the inner mental aspect of such processes. That aspect is what contributes value to being, what adds understanding to existence, what adds individual uniqueness to what otherwise might be universal processes, and what adds purposive direction to quasi-mechanical routines.

This is what after all Ryle himself believes. He says that when people concentrate on what they are doing, they do not perform two operations, but what they do has to be described "in terms of semi-dispositional, semi-episodic epithets".[2] He is not saying that human behaviour is just a series of "if-then" statements. There are inner episodes of attending, being careful, and so on. I think that it is slightly misleading, and that it actually did mislead Ryle on occasion, to say that these episodes "do not signify the concomitant occurrence of extra but internal operations".[3] For there are extra internal operations, which make a real causal difference to what happens in the external world – intelligent action is observably different from inattentive action. The point is that these internal operations and episodes are precisely the inner aspects of external operations, not intrusions or interferences from some other quite separate spirit-world.

Volitions and the will

Does the inner aspect of attending, concentrating, and intending make any causal difference to what happens in the world? The whole of human life assumes a positive answer. We are commanded to pay attention. We have to concentrate in order to improve our tennis strokes or our violin playing. We are blamed if we do not try our best. And we are usually praised if we try really hard, even if we fail. My school reports used to say: "He has done everything that we could have expected from him." Fortunately my parents always thought that was good, as they assumed that my teachers' expectations were high. I knew better, but I said nothing. The point is that my teachers did expect me to try, knew that what I did was limited by my abilities, but assumed that I could improve them by exerting a little more effort.

Education would be very different if we knew that everything people did was controlled by their brains and so could stick them into a brain scanner for half an hour and modify their brain states in the desired way, without them having to revise for days on end. Some schools seem to work on a principle rather like this, but we still think we can tell the difference between people whose brains have been efficiently modified by rote learning so that they know all the answers to standard examination questions and people who show originality and ingenuity, even though they have never even heard of the standard questions.

More importantly, perhaps, when it comes to moral issues, we assume that people generally know the difference between right and wrong and can stop doing wrong if they choose. There are exceptions of course. In France "crime passionnel" used to allow you to shoot your wife's lover if you found him in her bed. In England, however, this has never been allowed, since the English are expected to be able to control their passions or, more probably, it is assumed that they do not have any passions to control.

Ryle is adamant that there are no such things as "volitions", special mental acts that precede and cause physical acts. Yet of course he recognizes the difference between acting purposefully and acting inattentively or without thought. The difficulty is to capture that difference.

We should begin by recognizing that it is not brains who act, but persons. Persons have brains, just as they have fingernails, but neither fingernails nor brains act. A person is a very complex structure, including a brain, a body, a context of social relationships, and a place in history. Ryle stresses that we cannot count volitions. We do not know how many volitions we made this morning and whether they were hard or easy, painful or pleasant. But we cannot count how many actions we did this morning either. The mistake is not in positing mental acts. The mistake lies in thinking of mental acts as countable, discrete episodes.

The answer to the question "How many volitions did you have when you wrote this book?" is that that I was voliting continuously." There are no quanta of voliting. There is just a stream of volit, which I could split up in various ways. I can certainly decide to do something, but even then my decision may not be one identifiable action. It is a sort of redirection of attention, and it may occur over a long period of time.

It is a bit like asking, "When you were looking at that painting, how many looks did you have, and were some of them longer and more painful than others?" I probably looked at the painting for some time, more or less attentively. I certainly intended to look at it, which is to say that I directed my attention in a particular way. I am, when I am awake, continuously attending and intending. These are continuous mental processes. They are inner, if you like "occult", acts, though they normally have behavioural symptoms and perhaps always have correlative brain states.

The deepest argument for mental action is that without it there would be no knowledge of the world at all. Indeed, the world as a phenomenon would not exist. For I construct the phenomenal world as a sort of inner simulation of external reality. Some say that it is the brain that constructs such a reality-simulation. But they forget that the brain is part of the simulation. What appears to us as the brain is part of the phenomenal world that "we" construct. So the "we" cannot be the brain as it appears to any of us. It can, however, be the hidden reality of which the brain is an appearance, a reality not accessible to the senses, to which my conscious awareness of perceiving and thinking and feeling gives a distinctive mode of access.

That hidden reality, however, does not just consist of whatever gives rise to the physical brain. It is expressed in the brain as it exists in a specific body and in a wider social context and in a still wider set of historical and cultural occurrences. All these relationships go to make up that complex structure that gives rise to a simulation of reality, as it perceives and responds in feeling, evaluation, and action to the world from its own unique perspective.

When I say that persons act, I mean that there are centres of perception and innovation which exist within a many-layered web of physical, organic, personal, social, and historical relationships. They reflect that web from their own point of view, and they initiate changes in that web in response to their evaluations of what they perceive.

The brain has a central focal position in the web, but to simply concentrate on the correlations between brain and mental state as if they existed in isolation is to omit most of the rich complexity and diverse forms of relationship which go to form the content of mental states and the principles of causal change that are initiated within such complexes.

Perception itself is already a principle of causal change. It selects and integrates simulated sensory data from a surrounding environment. The fact that it occurs changes the causal, integrated, relational structure of which it is part. My perception of the world changes my response to the world. This happens continuously while consciousness exists.

Is this not just what Ryle thinks? In a way, yes. But not in the way he thinks. For he concentrates on the public, on the phenomenal, to the virtual exclusion of the private, which exists beyond the reach of sensory observation. Yet what is really important about persons, what we value about them, is their inner unique reflection of and response to the wider reality of which they are part. Persons have a unique series of experiences, which they integrate into their mental life in a unique way. That integration governs how new experiences are interpreted and builds up patterns of reactive action that become established as exercises of attention, practice, and achievement. The process is a continuous one of reception, integration, and response.

Persons are essentially responsive to a wider reality, not isolated in private asylums. They are essentially active causal agents in modifying that wider reality in response to their own perceptions and feelings. The inner life of a person is what drives the behaviour of a person. While it is correct to stress the vital importance of behaviour, of social context, and of active relationships within that context, it is radically misleading to deny that any unique inner perspective, evaluative feeling, and agency exist.

The inner life

Psychiatric counselling is the activity that most clearly reveals the importance of such an inner mental life. A good psychiatrist will try to empathize with patients, to be sensitive to what it is like to think and feel as they do. This requires a non-objective view of patients, an attempt to understand their inner lives, though without either approving of or condemning those lives. It takes years of training and skill to do this, and to make sense of the weird-sounding beliefs of some psychiatric patients demands a high degree of imagination and sensitivity. Yet the attempt can be made to understand how they see the world and interpret their experience, and why they see it as they do.

Sometimes, at least, patients can be encouraged to deal with their obsessions or neuroses by using specific techniques. They may be invited to take active control of their thoughts and habits, and it is assumed that they may be able to control such things. Psychiatrists know that there may be severe limits to such self-control, and sometimes there are physical pathologies of brain function that need to be dealt with medically. Nevertheless, an important area of self-analysis and reflection may remain, and to acknowledge that is part of respecting the proper personhood, the real if limited responsibility patients have for much of their mental lives.

Patients may be asked to consider their goals and the means to achieving them, and in that process they are invited to guide their thoughts (and thus their brain states) and actions by conscious focussing and effort. If such psychiatric counselling is valued at all, it presupposes that reflective thought can have a causal role in influencing future behaviour, whereas it would be considered invasive to simply modify the brain directly in a physical way, without attending to the wishes and desires of the patient.

There is no question that sometimes physical intervention with the brain is necessary. The brain can malfunction in many ways, and this may produce irrational thoughts and feelings. But we speak of behaviour being determined physically only when patients cannot exercise rational control, when there is something abnormal with their behaviour. In normal cases we assume that conscious thought can modify brain states, though we have no idea of the mechanics of this process.

But this is not unusual. We have no idea of the mechanics of how causes bring about effects in the publicly observable world either or of how it happens that causes are regularly followed by specific effects. That is just the way things are, and we have to accept it. The slightly different thing about thoughts causing brain states is that there is no public access to a person's thoughts, and there is no way of measuring thoughts quantitively. Thus we cannot set up equations describing the interactions of thought and brain, equations that could be checked experimentally. We cannot set up equations describing how brains give rise to thoughts either, but it is obvious to most of us that they do.

One way to think of this is to think of mental and physical events as two aspects of one composite reality, which taken together form a single whole. It is that single whole which is the causal complex that gives rise to the whole that succeeds it (the effect). It seems natural that the causal properties of such a composite whole will be significantly different from the causal properties of non-sentient matter, not organized in such a way as to generate mental events.

At the simple inorganic level there are very regular and repetitive laws, which can be plotted, at least in relatively isolated situations, with a high degree of simplicity and predictive accuracy. This simple scheme breaks down at the subatomic level, where indeterminacy and entanglement introduce much more complicated factors. But it operates at the level of everyday observations, where wave-functions collapse into observable events. At the level of highly structured brain states, operating in organic bodies and rapidly changing social contexts, the operation of laws is much looser and permits novel, unique, and unpredictable occurrences. Subjective evaluations and a relatively free choice of goals, social constraints, and learned and modifiable behaviour patterns become factors that economists and social scientists have to take into account in explaining human conduct.

It is not that ethereal minds follow one set of laws (where evaluations, reasons, and goals rule), and brains follow another set of laws (where only charge, mass, and spin rule), and each must in some mysterious way mesh with the other. Rather, when complex brains come to exist and operate properly, the sorts of laws that govern their behaviour expand to include new factors of subjective evaluation, creative response, and empathetic relationship. Rocks and planets do not evaluate things, adjust their behaviour accordingly, and react to the perceived feelings and purposes of other rocks. Rocks have no feelings or purposes. But people, complex organized physical organisms, do. There are not two separate worlds. There is one world, existing at various levels of emergent complexity. At the higher levels, the behaviour of objects is modified by the presence of feelings and purposes, which add new causal influences that shape the immediate future states of that part of the world.

Ryle puts this by speaking of the "bogy of mechanism". The ghost is not in the machine; it is in the thought that the universe is a machine. Mechanical laws only apply to a certain sub-class of physical events – namely, mechanical events. But there are lots

of non-mechanical events, including, most obviously, people, who
are not machines. So "the discoveries of the physical sciences no
more rule out life, sentience, purpose or intelligence from presence
in the world than do the rules of grammar extrude style or logic
from prose".[4] Exactly so. Unfortunately, Ryle goes on to say that
sentience and purpose do not imply extra entities which have any
causal properties – that would, he thinks, be dualism, a very horrid
thing.

Yet an intention is often an occurrent thought that causes
physical changes to occur, and sentience is almost always a set of
occurrent feelings and perceptions that affect the way observers
behave. Thoughts and feelings are parts of the complex whole from
which an immediately succeeding state is generated. They make a
difference to what happens next.

Ryle argues that it is not true that I first of all do something
(have a thought) which causes my body to act. For then my doing
something mental would have to be preceded by an earlier act that
caused me to do that thing, and so on ad infinitum. But that is not
so. Not all my doings have to be preceded by prior doings. I can
just do some things straight away (Ryle obviously agrees, because
he says so). Very often, though not always, what I do straight away
is form a thought about what I might do next. Not all my acts
need to be preceded by theorizing explicitly. But some do, when I
wonder what I am going to do next. Such wondering often does
take place, and it involves some occurrent yet occult acts, which
can issue in a later physical action (though it may not, since I may
change my mind). There is no infinite regress here, just the fact that
sometimes I think before I act, though quite often, unfortunately,
I do not.

Ryle and I agree that it is misleading to speak of minds as
knowing propositions and producing hidden volitions in a quite
separate mental world, which is then mysteriously causally
connected to this physical world, in which the body resides.
We agree also that it is very important to see human beings as
intelligent agents with purposes and values, living in a social world,

More than Matter

developing or failing to develop their abilities and dispositions, and interacting with others, whom they know more or less well. We disagree about whether our ordinary human actions in the world have a vitally important aspect which is private, capable of being completely hidden from others, and which has an important causal influence on some purely physical movements. And we disagree about whether philosophical reflection can cast any light on this mental aspect by bringing out its metaphysical foundations and implications or whether philosophy simply asks us to attend closely to how we actually apply words to observable human behaviour. Behind these differences lies a different view of what human persons are, and of what the place of consciousness, value, and purpose is in the world. I think Ryle's rejection of materialism and mechanism, and his affirmation of distinctive human values, is entirely correct. My only complaint is that he does not bring out the philosophical underpinning of the humanist understanding he wishes to defend. In the end, an appeal to common sense is too arbitrary and insubstantial to support a totally humanist view.

Chapter Twelve

Minds and moral values

Feelings are not just, as Ryle seems to say, tickles, urges, and tinglings. They are our deepest forms of response to the world in which we find ourselves, and they are closely connected with our most basic evaluations and active responses. As Aristotle said, what is distinctive of human personhood is the ability to pursue human excellence in relation to what is good — that is, the pursuit of virtue. The distinctive virtues of a human life are intelligent freedom and creativity, conscious appreciation and understanding, and the fostering of social cooperation and compassion. These are the objects of intelligent and informed moral choice, and they involve the cultivation of feelings that can more fully realize the possibilities of a good human life.

In this chapter and the next I want to explore further just what it is about the inner lives of human persons that gives them unique moral value; what enables them to live a genuinely human life, a life that is good for human persons as such. I want to argue that it is very largely their capacity to have a rich and complex feeling-life, in which states and objects are felt and evaluated, and become the basis for intentionally aiming at future goals. Moreover, this is not just a matter of purely subjective feelings, which can vary indefinitely between different people. There are some objective goals that are rationally worthy of choice, and the moral uniqueness of human persons lies in the ability to choose or to ignore such goals. Without the capacity to feel, to evaluate, and to choose future goals, humans would not be the morally responsible agents, worthy of special respect and compassion, that most of us take them to be. Human moral dignity does not lie, as many materialists suppose, in pursuing actions that have proved conducive to survival in the long evolutionary past of humanity. It lies in the capacity to choose goals of action that are (whatever their past or present relevance to survival) objectively good, and that are known to be good by rational reflection upon inner human experience. That is why an affirmation of dualism (or dual-aspect idealism, as I have called it) is of the greatest practical importance.

I believe that almost everything that we value about human beings belongs to our inner lives. Of course we like having bodies, and we are very sorry when bits of them do not work. But even then what is important about bodies is that they give us pleasure or pain – conscious feelings – and they enable us to perform some interesting activities and pursue some of our purposes and desires.

Everybody would prefer to be happy than to be in intense pain – well, almost everybody. For most of the time, and for most people, pain is bad. So straight away we find that good reasons for action involve feelings of pleasure and pain. It is reasonable to avoid pain and seek pleasure; pain is bad and pleasure is good – that, for most people, is just obvious.

I do not think that seeking pleasure and avoiding pain are the only good reasons for action, by any means. Such a view fails to distinguish personal, human life from that of other animals. But the notion of reasons for action only begins to make sense when some form of consciousness – minimally, sentience, or the capacity for feeling pleasure and pain – exists.

Some philosophers think that is all there is to morality. Jeremy Bentham, who had himself stuffed and put on show at University College, London, once said that the only good reason for acting was to seek pleasure and avoid pain. Presumably he thought that seeing him stuffed would make a lot of people very happy.

The best hope of personal happiness may lie in fulfilling our natures as human beings, as essentially related and interdependent and social agents. We are not machines that accumulate as many units of pleasure as possible, and who see other human machines as competing pleasure-units who are primarily useful to us as providers of our own pleasure.

We like things, states or activities that make us happy. But, as Ryle says, there is not one thing called happiness that we can seek just for its own sake. When I enjoy gardening, I do not experience two distinct things: gardening and a feeling of pleasure. I feel pleasure in gardening. But of course pleasure does exist in addition to digging behaviour. It is the subjective feeling I have when I dig. I certainly know the difference between having that feeling and not having it when digging on a cold and rainy day.

People feel pleased or disgusted by different things. Bentham hoped that we could measure pleasure and so calculate just how much pleasure any action might bring to everybody concerned. But, he said, "Pushpin (pool or snooker) is as good as poetry." Five units of pleasure from lying in a jacuzzi is five times as pleasant as one unit of pleasure from reading Dostoevsky. This finding may seem to be corroborated by the unfortunate (or perhaps very happy) monkeys who had their brains electrically stimulated to produce orgasms whenever they pressed a red button on a desk in front of them. What happened was that they pressed the red button repeatedly all day until they were completely exhausted. But maybe that was because they couldn't read Dostoevsky.

Orgasms may be very pleasant. But even Jeremy Bentham might hesitate at the thought that we ought to aim at the greatest number of orgasms for the greatest number of people. Most philosophers tend to agree with that other great utilitarian philosopher, John Stuart Mill, that the "higher pleasures", pleasures of the mind, are worth more than sensual pleasures. They engage the mind; they require learning and practice; they require concentration and skill; they extend understanding and creativity; and they seem to be worthwhile in themselves, not to be just ways of filling in the time. Even orgasms, for many of us, are enriched when they occur in the context of a relationship of genuine love and personal commitment. They are not just bodily sensations.

Whatever arguments may be used to speak of distinctively human pleasures, they essentially involve types of human consciousness and understanding, in which feelings of many different sorts are involved. Feelings are, as Ryle rightly said, specified by their objects, by the sorts of activities that evoke them. Such activities are often chosen because of the feelings associated with them. To the extent this is true, the feelings that only an individual can experience are real elements of reality, with real causal influence. They add a vital element to observable behaviour, and they belong to the inner life of socially engaged human animals.

Gilbert Ryle's peculiar feelings

Gilbert Ryle was basically an Aristotelian, who agreed that true happiness is to be found in the exercise of distinctively human skills and excellences (in the pursuit of virtue, as Aristotle put it). Strangely, however, when Ryle came to say what feelings were, he provided the following list: "thrills, twinges, pangs, throbs, wrenches, itches, prickings, chills, glows, loads, qualms, hankerings, curdlings, sinkings, tensions, gnawing and shocks".[1] One can only assume that his inner life was a succession of more or less alarming episodes of chronic indigestion.

"How are you feeling?" we can imagine his colleagues at Magdalen College asking. "This morning," he might reply, "I had three twinges, a small curdling, and two throbs." If he did, we might imagine them backing away with a slightly alarmed expression. This is certainly a very odd list of feelings. When listening to Mozart, one may be overcome by feeling, without being able to identify any pangs or itches.

The "myth of feeling" that Ryle opposes is the myth that feelings occur in some hidden world, and that they cause actions in the physical world to occur. Whereas, he says, feelings or emotions are primarily dispositions to behave in certain ways. Dispositions are not causes. To be vain, for example, is to be liable to say vain things and to parade around in front of people when the opportunity arises.

It is true that there is not such a thing as a feeling of vanity that may unexpectedly descend upon you when you are walking down the street and that suddenly causes you to say things like, "What a handsome person I am." Vanity is a personality trait, a disposition to say vain things, to preen yourself in the mirror, and so on. But part of this behavioural disposition is that when you look at yourself in the mirror, you do have a feeling of pleasure in your own handsomeness. Those feelings may not be causes of your behaviour, but they are important parts of being vain. Vanity is not in itself a feeling, but there are feelings of vanity, which may be characterized as the sort of feelings you are apt to have when you think unduly well of yourself in relation to other people.

Ryle is right; feelings are not usually causes. Yet he is wrong to imply that feelings are not occurrences that are quite different from physical behaviour, and that are very important to a person's life. Such feelings are part of a very complex integration of many factors – the brain is in specific states. The body exhibits physical symptoms and behaves in characteristic ways. That body exists in a specific social and historical context, which makes evaluative comparisons with other people possible – the vain fop must have the belief that he is better than others, he must perceive himself in a specific way, and then there must be that sort of "puffed up" feeling that consists in the felt awareness that one is better than others. The cause of vanity, insofar as there is one, is a specific sort of awareness in a social context, which gives rise to evaluative beliefs that have a felt emotional quality, a distinctive sort of pleasure that is naturally expressed in bodily sensations and physical behaviour of a peculiarly obnoxious kind (to others).

It is the evaluative element that is important to feelings and emotions. We feel pity if we feel pain at the suffering of others, and evaluate such suffering as bad and to be avoided where possible. Pity is a very natural feeling. It involves the perception of another, the belief that they are suffering, and the evaluation that it would be better for them if they were not. The feeling of pity is the felt awareness of another's suffering, coupled with some desire to alleviate it if possible. There is good reason to seek states that bring pleasure and avoid states that bring pain. But one kind of pain is the pain you may feel at the perception of another's suffering. Humans are so bound together as social animals that good humour is infectious, and so is sorrow. We are well aware of how one person can cheer up a whole gathering, while another person might spoil any part by their depressed utterances. It would be very hard to have a great party while one of the guests was noisily expiring in a corner. There may be sadomasochistic parties where that would be regarded as adding to the fun. But they are not the norm. Because most of us are taught to laugh by our mothers and soothed by them when we feel pain, it is entirely natural to respond to the happiness or gloom of others by mirroring their state in ourselves.

In our emotional inner lives we naturally appreciate beauty of various sorts and are repelled by certain smells and sensations. When we perceive the mental states of others – and Ryle is entirely correct to say that we do so normally by interpreting their behaviour – we appreciate their happiness or intellectual acumen, and we are repelled by their pain or vanity. There is a social dimension to most feelings, as we evaluate the evaluations that are made by others (we see that they dislike pain, and so we dislike their pain too).

The emotional lives of humans are governed by the evaluations we make of the complex world we encounter in awareness (perception interpreted by thought). That world includes the dispositions and intentions and feelings of other persons and of ourselves. Our evaluations are not arbitrarily subjective – that is, they are not correlated contingently with the objects of awareness. We do not see the aurora borealis and say, "What a horrible green mess." Of course we might. It is reported of Dr Johnson that when he first saw a hillside of gorgeous heather fully in bloom in Scotland, he simply said, "What horrid blotchy purple hills." There is no accounting for taste. But we can learn to appreciate purple and many other things too. Or at least generations of musicians and artists and literary theorists think and hope we can.

To dislike the music of Wagner is one thing. But to say that it is trivial or superficial or devoid of merit is another. You can learn Wagner's place in musical history, how harmonic traditions grew more complex, and how Wagner developed one operatic tradition to express it in a richer way, which was outstandingly excellent of its kind – and you can still not bear to listen to *The Ring*. But you would have to say that it displays outstanding excellence, and that it develops a tradition in a profoundly creative and distinctive way. You may not like that tradition – but you will have to admit that others do and are deeply moved by the music, and that it meets superbly certain criteria of excellence, which you may not like very much.

There are seemingly irreducible differences of taste. For decades no one liked the music of J. S. Bach, and then he became, for many, the greatest of all musicians. Who is right and who is wrong? Or is everyone's opinion as good as everyone else's? Maybe these are the wrong questions. The fact is that some people will never like Bach – too austere, too intellectual, too tuneless, some would say (except for one or two favourite pieces). Yet there is much to appreciate in Bach, and you can be taught to appreciate it better if you have the initial "feeling for it".

It is a bit like wine-tasting. Some people will never drink wine. Some do not like it. Some like it, but cannot tell which wines are good and which bad. But we might all admit that some people have a more discriminating palate, and can distinguish between

different vintages of the same wine with no difficulty. They are the
people we would consult if we had an initial interest in wine. They
are the experts, even if they are experts in areas that nobody else is
interested in (like philosophy).

So maybe the bottom line is this: you cannot help your initial
feelings, your basic likes and inclinations. But you can cultivate
them and have a "refined palate" or a "refined musical taste" – and
then you might get a job as a wine or music critic. Of course
different critics will still disagree very strongly about many things.
But they will, however grudgingly, have to accept that there
are degrees of expertise, of knowledge, experience, and skill in
appreciating wine or music or art.

In these areas, strong disagreement and generally accepted
degrees of skill or competence go together. I have to admit –
I gladly admit – that Gilbert Ryle was a learned, wise, skilful,
and innovative philosopher. But I think he was blind to the rich
evaluative and emotional life of human beings, and so I disagree
strongly with some of his conclusions about such things.

What makes human life worthwhile is our rich emotional
inner life. Our perceptions are integrated and interpreted by
thought, evaluated by feeling, and responded to by intention and
creative action, within a social community of other beings with
thoughts, feelings, and intentions. It is interpretative thought,
evaluative feeling, creative intention, and cooperative empathy
that distinguish human persons as autonomous moral agents and
give to human life a special sort of value. Such a thought may,
thank goodness, be implicit in much common-sense thought. But
it can be undermined by a critical reason that overlooks or even
denies the importance of the subjective personal life of feeling
and intention. To that extent, Ryle's objections to Cartesian
dualism may, however unintentionally, undermine a reasonable
commitment to the moral value of human personhood. For such
commitment is founded on a perception of the moral priority of
the embodied mind.

The objectivity of values

Ryle says, "A person can usually... tell without research whether he enjoys something... but so can his associates."[2] What is right about this is that we naturally express our thoughts and feelings in our behaviour and in the things we say. Yet our behaviour may be misleading, and what we say often does not express what we mean. There may often be no behaviour at all – which is why, when I am thinking deeply and profoundly, my wife thinks I have gone to sleep. Also, our feelings vary in tone and intensity. They can inhibit or enhance our actions, but no one else can know just how intense my feelings are or what their complexity and quality is.

Undeterred, Ryle goes on to say that if we want to find out about our feelings when they are concealed, other people are more likely to succeed than we are. It is true that we often deceive ourselves and do not admit that we are vain or ambitious or aggressive. But these are, as Ryle says, not so much feelings as dispositions or character traits, and we often conceal our characters from ourselves – probably because we do not like ourselves very much. We can, however, practice self-knowledge and explore what our feelings are like in ways that others cannot. Admittedly we do not have many linguistic resources for doing so. If I look into myself and try to describe my feeling-state at this moment, I may say something rather feeble, like "There is a pang of contentment, with a few twinges of lassitude around the edges, a dollop of resolution, and two throbs of anticipation."

That is why introspective psychology came to a halt in the early twentieth century – people just didn't have the words to describe what they felt. And when they did describe, it was of no scientific use – it did not help to predict or explain causally. It just reported, in very boring ways, what was going on in someone's mind. Some philosophers concluded that there was nothing to describe or that "what went on inside" was irrelevant. But poets and novelists, musicians and artists, manage better by finding ways to express feelings that communicate in a special way to others or at least to those who are initially sympathetic. Even the most peculiar examples of modern art express a personal vision of the world that communicates a certain feeling toward it. That feeling could be one of disgust or alienation or sadomasochism, which is why art is so powerful. It communicates a feeling, evaluative response that is part of the artist's awareness and personal interpretation of the world and that arouses a responsive (not identical) feeling in those who are able to resonate with it.

Feelings differ enormously in different people and are not separable from individual awareness, interpretation, and responsive actions. We cannot sensibly aim at having feelings as discrete items isolated from the states or activities they are feelings about – that is the utilitarian mistake. Yet without feelings we would be automata, and it would be hard to give any value to human awareness or any purpose to human actions. Human life is largely concerned with the kinds of feelings we seek or avoid, with the activities that evoke or sustain them, and with the social relationships that enrich or destroy them.

Are feelings of this sort just matters of purely personal taste? Or are there some feelings that would be accepted by all reasonable people as bad and others that are good?

In the arts it is difficult to claim that there are absolute standards of good and bad – though we can distinguish different levels of skill, originality of vision, creativity, and expertise in a specific tradition or style. Within classical harmonic music, Mozart stands out as particularly skilful, original, and expressive of profound feeling. Anyone who appreciates that sort of classical music should be able to recognize Mozart as an outstanding composer. Within a particular tradition of creative art, there are standards of excellence that it would be insensitive not to appreciate. But we are perhaps prepared to accept that some people simply do not like classical music. So objective evaluations do exist in the arts, but they are tradition-specific, and it does not make much sense to say that classical music is better than romantic music or jazz. That is why it does not make sense to say that anyone, even Mozart, is "the best composer ever".

He is the master of a specific style, but we are not required or expected to appreciate every style of music there ever was.

There are some things, however, which every reasonable person has a good reason to avoid. It would be hard to understand someone who said, "I am really looking forward to an agonizing toothache." If some religious fanatic said that, we might understand that he thinks if he endures the toothache he will get some great heavenly reward. Even then he would not look forward to the toothache for its own sake, and if he did not think it was a necessary means to some greater good, he would soon change his mind.

Religious fanatics apart, we would expect everyone to think that agonizing pains are to be avoided wherever possible. That is to say that pain is bad. It is objectively bad – every being that can feel pain has a good reason to avoid it, and if we care about other beings at all, we have reason to help them avoid it. Why should we care about other beings? We don't always. Little boys routinely torture insects or small animals. But because we are social animals, we do care about some other beings, if only our own children or parents. We find happiness in making them happy, on birthdays and holidays. Even if we do not care about people we have never met, we can see that they have a reason to avoid pain, and we have no reason to cause them pain, unless it will produce some good for us (which, alas, it often does).

Other things than pain are objectively bad. There are very good reasons to avoid ignorance, since ignorance can lead us to make disastrous mistakes. There are good reasons to avoid powerlessness, which can cause us to fall prey to the whims of the powerful. There are good reasons to avoid hating other people, since that will usually cause them to hate and harm us if they can.

These are not absolutes. Sometimes we may prefer to be ignorant – about the time of our death or about our chances of getting diabetes, for instance. We may prefer to be slaves, if we can get a fairly easy life with a lax slave-owner. We may successfully hate other people, if we can terrify them into doing what we want. Nevertheless, in general and for most of us pain, ignorance, slavery, and hatred are things to be avoided. They are prima facie evils — things which in general there are good reasons to avoid.

Where there are prima facie evils, there must be prima facie goods. Pleasure, knowledge, freedom, and sympathetic feeling are objective goods. We will train children to seek them, and will reckon that most people will have a happy life if they achieve them or a reasonable degree of them.

These are very general values, and in human lives they will be filled out in a huge variety of ways. As I have noted, pleasure is not one thing that everyone will pursue in the same way. Happiness is to be found in many mental states and in many activities, and such states will be very diverse. But it is not an accident that knowledge, freedom, and sympathetic feeling are objective values, things that humans have a good reason to pursue and sustain. For these values point to the distinctive character of human consciousness. They are states or acts that make us fully and distinctively human. If we lack them, our distinctive humanity is impaired. A suffering, ignorant slave who hates everyone is a diminished human being, not exercising the capacities that make humans what they are. It may not be the slave's fault, but it is still a life that is objectively frustrated in many ways. Conversely, a happy, wise, free, and compassionate person is living a life which is fully human, because it exercises the capacities that are distinctive of human beings.

Human animals, supremely among all species on earth, are capable of abstract intellectual understanding and of delight in beauty and in artistic artefacts. They are able to be creative in their thoughts and actions, transforming their environment in new ways. They are able to empathize with the feelings of others, and to cooperate in learning and in action, so that they can share in the experiences of others and work jointly with them to devise new cultural projects.

These capacities are not discrete and isolated from one another. They are intertwined, so that understanding and appreciation of beauty are creative acts that involve cooperation with others. They suggest an ideal for human personhood that consists, as

166

Aristotle put it, in the unimpeded exercise of distinctively human capacities. To understand and appreciate fully, to act creatively, to be compassionate, and to cooperate with others – these are the virtues of a genuinely human life. Each human being is born into a unique situation and faces problems and possibilities never shared in detail with anyone else. Nevertheless, there are goals for human life as such, and in every historically particular situation the mind can be disciplined to love those excellences that are distinctive to human personhood.

Chapter Thirteen

Acting for the sake
of good alone

*In the end, the essential capacity of human persons
is the capacity to choose the good for its own sake
(in Christian terms, to love God with mind and
heart and strength). The privacy of inner experience
and the importance of introspection and growth in
self-knowledge is of crucial moral importance for
human personhood. That is why Ryle's attack on
dualism, implicitly on idealism, and on the inner
life as primarily distinctive of human personhood,
despite its many insights, should be resisted.*

If we are disposed to think of mind as having ontological priority,
it will be natural to think of the fullest development of mind as the
innate goal of human history or even of the cosmic process as a
whole. Human beings could well be only one of many forms that
personhood or mind takes in the cosmos. But the development of
personal powers embodied in a particular species – *homo sapiens* –
provides an objective goal for human life and feeling.

The goal is founded upon the distinctive capacities of human nature, which characterize what is rationally good and desirable for a being with such capacities, and what is bad or diminishing and is to be avoided. This moral ideal is concerned with feelings, but feelings considered as integrated with social and personal activities, with knowledge and understanding, and with rational evaluations of envisaged states and acts. Feelings are not, in other words, twinges, tingles, and throbs. They are affective and reactive evaluations based on inner experience of the complex world with which we consciously interact. They give to human lives a sense of value and a sense of purpose (to realize objective values), which is perhaps the most important and distinctive feature of being human.

Mental discipline is not easy. Knowledge may be a good thing, but anyone who has taught in school knows that it is quite hard to get some pupils to learn. Interests and abilities vary enormously, and some lack the interest to learn very much. They may also lack the motivation and application that is necessary to learn. Moreover, humans are very prone to exaggeration, gossip, and rumour. Lies and misinformation spread easily, and very few of us have the time and patience to gain full information even about topics we are interested in. The ideal might be truth, but the reality is often a mixture of hearsay, deceit, and ignorance. Even those who sincerely seek for truth can have a very limited view of where truth is to be found and of the best way of finding it.

Some religious movements, for instance, think that believers must be prevented from reading anything that would disturb their beliefs. That attitude is not confined to religion. Ruling political parties may "massage the truth" so that it presents a one-sided and distorted message, and they may censor opposing opinions. In fact, it is entirely typical of human communication in general that it distorts truth and propagates prejudice and hatred.

Why should people lie? That is simple. Lies are usually more interesting than the truth. The imaginary adventures of Baron Munchausen are much more interesting than the daily drudge of an assembly-line worker. People like good storytellers. And if the storyteller can claim to be the hero of his own stories, this will add considerably to his reputation. Good liars can increase their social status enormously, as long as they are not found out – which usually requires a constant stream of even bigger lies to conceal the much less interesting truth.

Really big liars will do almost anything to prevent being found out. In such a world the pursuit of truth may be difficult, even dangerous. Partly for that reason, some people who wish to pursue truth try to leave the world behind and live in relatively closed societies where truth of a certain sort is valued. Unfortunately, this policy does not really work, for most truths have to be discovered precisely in that ambiguous social world where truth and deceit are inextricably mixed up. The renunciation of secular knowledge is not, after all, a very reliable path to knowing as much about reality as possible. It is possible that cloistered contemplation does disclose very important facts about the inner life of the mind, about mindfulness, equanimity, and universal compassion, for instance. But it does not disclose much about quantum physics or genetic mutation. If we are really to comprehend the world in its fullness, we must know both about our inner lives and about the nature of the world, including the evil that is in it. The life of meditation may be one way of discovering truth, but it cannot be the only way. The pursuit of the human ideal of comprehension of truth involves many different kinds of knowing. We may only be able to pursue some, but we should not deny the existence of the others, and we should encourage their pursuit as much as we can.

The quest for truth, then, is difficult and often requires prolonged struggle against strong opposition. The same is true of the search for the other basic personal values – of appreciation, creativity, compassion, and cooperation. They require effort and sometimes sacrifice in a world filled with indifference, the will to power, hatred, and conflict. It is not surprising that a fully human life is rare and attained only by few. Is it reasonable to demand it of any human being?

Many philosophers have held that there is an ultimate moral

choice in every human life. We can choose what is good for its own sake or we can choose what is good for us, regardless of others. We can put goodness first or we can put ourselves first. Reason cannot decide between these choices. Neither can desire, for we must decide which of our desires to follow. Nor can the choice be seen as an arbitrary decision of will, without cause or reason, for such a choice would be absurd. No, we decide whether to subordinate ourselves to the good or to subordinate the good to ourselves. That choice determines the sort of person we are, and so is of fundamental importance to our lives, yet no further reason can be given for it than that one ought to choose the good (or alternatively that one ought to choose one's own long-term good). This is the truth behind Kant's dictum that we must do our duty for its own sake.

Duty and desire

Kant is often misunderstood on this point. He is supposed to have said that you only know you are doing your duty if you act in opposition to your own desires. Otherwise you might be acting in accordance with desire, not because it is your duty. So you are only really good if you are doing what you do not want to do. It is as if you are really desperate for a drink, yet you know you ought not to drink because you are going to drive. Being English, you pass a pub every few yards. Every time you come to a pub, you have a huge craving for a drink, and you have a huge struggle to overcome that craving. After a few heart-stopping minutes, the sense of duty wins, though the struggle leaves you emotionally exhausted. Heaving a sigh of relief, you walk on – only to come to another pub, where the same process takes place again. By the time you get to your car, nine pubs later, you are a quivering wreck. Having done this every day for a week, you might decide it is better never to go out at all. Except that it might be your duty to go out. So every day you have a nerve-racking struggle about whether to leave the house or not.

To be fair to Kant, he did warn against "moral fanaticism", which is the mistake of letting your life be filled with crucial moral decisions. As Aristotle said, it is better just to become the sort of person who is habitually good. Then you can pass all the pubs with equanimity, because, once you have made a firm decision not to drink and drive, you are not even tempted to have a drink.

Kant said that it was just about impossible to tell if you were acting from a purely moral motive (because it is right) or from long-term selfish desire. Maybe we should not agonize about that, but just get on with trying to do things because it is right to do so, without worrying about what our deepest motives are. There are people who will say that all human actions are really self-interested. Even if we give all our money to the poor, we really do so because we gain some inner satisfaction or some social approval from doing so. You can never refute that argument. But you could equally well say that all our selfish actions are really altruistic, because they are aimed at the happiness of someone who does not yet exist. I exist now, but people who exist in the future are not identical to me, and so even my selfish actions are aimed at someone other than me (some future person who happens to share some memories and character traits with me and who happens to have a body very like mine), which is a form of altruism. I don't suppose that argument seems very convincing, but it is no worse than the argument that the more altruistic I try to be, the more selfish I actually am.

The upshot seems to be that reasoning can tell me what things are good, in general. But the decision to do things because they are good is not made either by more reasonable people or by people who just happen to have the most altruistic desires. Moral action is not unreasonable, and it is not necessarily opposed to desire. But it is quite distinct from both reason and desire. It is a basic option that determines what sort of person you are.

It was for this reason that Kant felt it would actually be harmful if you knew there was a life after death, where you would be judged for what you had done during this life. That, he thought, would turn moral action into long-term prudence, and so it would undermine the whole point of morality. You have to do your duty without thought of personal reward. In fact, if you do things out of self-interest, you will go to hell. So everybody who does things because they want to go to heaven will land up in hell. And only people who do not care whether they go to heaven or not will get there. It seems that hell will be full of people who have spent their lives trying to get to heaven, while heaven will be full of people who do not particularly want to be there. There must be something wrong somewhere.

Kant's suggestion actually is that you should do things because they are right. But it is all right to *hope* that it will make you happy in the long run, as long as that is not your main motive. He even, notoriously perhaps, argued that the hope for "happiness-in-accordance-with-virtue" was a condition of the possibility of rational moral action. Perhaps that is a way of saying that it is pointless to aim at a just society if such a thing will always remain impossible. A reasonable action will only aim at something that is at least possible, even if very difficult.

But the reply to that is that moral action can always make things better than they would have been, even if it will never achieve a perfect society (whatever that would be). If the world is like that, it is tragic — good people will often die in vain, unknown, unrecognized, and unappreciated. Naturally, we would wish the world not to be tragic. That is probably one major motivation for some religious beliefs. It does not make such beliefs true, but it may at least ground them in reasonable and humane and comprehensible human desires, rather than in irrational, vindictive or self-centred motivations.

It may be said that Kant makes an unduly subtle distinction between hoping for heaven and believing that there is a heaven. If you can hope for heaven without undermining your moral motivation, then surely you can believe there is a heaven without making that your main motivation for acting. After all, even believing that there is a heaven is not absolute theoretical certainty. It is a belief that may easily be mistaken. And that may be Kant's main point – though even then I am not sure that absolute theoretical certainty about rewards and punishments would make it impossible to act purely for the sake of goodness. It would just make it more difficult to distinguish that from long-term prudence. It is a relief to find that religious people can be really good and also to find that non-religious people can be genuinely good too, just because they feel goodness is worth aiming at for its own sake, and that a genuinely human life is one that acts for the sake of good alone.

That is the main conclusion of this chapter, which has been chiefly concerned to affirm that the capacity to act for the sake of goodness, and for no other reason, is one of the most important capacities of human persons. That capacity cannot be reduced to, or exhaustively described in terms of, any genetic account of how moral awareness originated through evolution or any purely material description of what human beings are. The commandingness of morality requires an affirmation of the uniquely individual appropriation of inner experience and the responsible freedom of moral agents. That requires that human persons are more than matter, and in that "more" lies the significance and meaning of their lives.

Inner experience as evidence for idealism

Part of Ryle's goal is to escape from what he thinks of as the Cartesian myth that each person has a totally private and hidden mind which has to be inferred from bodily movements in a completely uncheckable way. Ryle suggests that humans are not either ghosts or machines, much less ghosts in machines. They are social animals. Their minds as well as their bodies have a physical, genetic, evolutionary history, which is an important component of what they are. And humans are essentially social, finding themselves in a particular society with a unique history and culture, and defining themselves in relation to other people with whom they continually and directly interact.

So far so good (except that Descartes did not himself believe the "Cartesian myth"). But humans are also essentially morally responsible agents, capable of pursuing goodness for its own sake and of shaping both the world and their own characters in the light of their moral ideals – or, more often, failing to do so. They have a rich inner life, in which understanding, feeling, evaluation, and intention play a major role, a life and quality of experience which is not open to others to inspect.

This inner life is known by introspection, by a form of self-examination which inspects a person's feelings, beliefs, evaluations, and motives without the use of the senses. Introspection is non-sensory knowledge of one's own states of mind, and it is an important part of coming to know if and to what extent and in what ways one is pursuing a life which is wholly good.

It is quite difficult to work out exactly what Ryle thinks of introspection. He did not really like being called a behaviourist – someone who denies that there are any causally relevant mental states – though he thought it was a fairly harmless appellation. And he speaks of "semi-episodic" dispositional states, which include talking to oneself or knowing that one has a toothache. But he leaves a strong impression that such inner states are parasitic upon observable bodily states, like talking to others or crying out in pain, and that they are not of primary importance in human life.

This impression is strongest when he speaks of mental images, the existence of which he seems flatly to deny. I would sit in his study and say, "I am now having a mental image of Big Ben." "No you are not," he would reply. "You are just imagining that you are seeing Big Ben. You are pretending to see it. There is no image there. There cannot be any image, because there is nowhere for it to be. It is not inside your skull, and it is certainly not in front of your eyes, because I can see what is in front of your eyes, and there is nothing there. This supposed image is nowhere. And that is not surprising, because you are just imagining that it is there."

It was very hard to think of a satisfactory reply, since I was sitting there having the mental image, and Ryle simply couldn't see it. Of course he couldn't. It was a mental image after all, and he wasn't supposed to see it. But how could he deny that I was seeing it? He was quite right that I was just imagining that I was seeing Big Ben. That is what having a mental image of Big Ben is! I did not think I was magically transported to London and was standing in front of the clock tower. I pretended that I was in London, looking at Big Ben. But I was not looking at the actual thing. I was constructing a picture of Big Ben, without actually drawing and without leaving my armchair. And there was something there – a mentally constructed picture of Big Ben, in full colour. I was imagining it. But there was an object that I imagined, and it was an object that only I could observe, not with my physical eyes, and not in any publicly observable space.

Ryle was so opposed to the idea of a private inner space that he had the confidence to tell me that I was not really having a mental image when I quite clearly was. As a matter of fact, I could also hear music "in my head", but I did not tell him that, as he might have given me an aspirin and called a doctor.

I am quite convinced that I have non-sensory knowledge of mental images both visual and auditory, including dreams, and that I also have thoughts and feelings that I am careful never to tell anyone about. Ryle seemed to think that I could tell anyone about them if I chose, and that I could not know anything about them if I had not first learned from others what my thoughts and feelings were. In addition, other people are better at knowing what my thoughts and feelings are than I am. All these claims seem to me to be mistaken.

Hidden knowledge

There is, as usual, something important in what Ryle says. One main purpose of self-examination is to review your behaviour in the recent past and ask if it was motivated by selfish interests or if it was genuinely altruistic and compassionate. It is true that others may see aspects of our behaviour that we might miss. We are mostly prejudiced in our own favour and tend to put our behaviour in the best possible light. It is true that it is not easy to see ourselves honestly, and that we repress many feelings and motives that may be obvious to others, but that we disguise from ourselves. Psychiatrists exist partly in order to make this very clear.

Nevertheless not all our behaviour is overt. The "smiling depressive", for example, is someone who shows no outward signs of depression at all, but who may unexpectedly try to take their own lives, to the surprise and consternation of their friends. We might be well-advised to keep many of our thoughts and daydreams, many of our hopes and ambitions, to ourselves. While we may often disguise them, some of them are obvious enough to us, but to no one else. As Machiavelli pointed out, the wish to be rich and famous is best hidden from others, while we publicly express only the desire to help others and to bring about world peace. Successful hypocrisy is never discovered; it is only that most of us are not very good at it. But practice makes perfect, and if we try really hard, we can probably manage it.

It is not that we have perfect knowledge of our own feelings, while others have no access to them at all. We normally do express our feelings in observable ways, and we often do not recognize our own feelings for what they really are. We learn to formulate our thoughts about such feelings in language we have learned from others, and that may be felt inadequate for what we want to convey. Nevertheless, we do have a mode of access to our feelings and thoughts that no one else has. That mode of access is non-sensory, and it is required for full knowledge of a person. Without it, we would not be able to discipline ourselves in the love of virtue, and our lives could not be completely centred on the good and beautiful, as they could and ought to be.

We would not believe someone who said, "I know the answer to this mathematical problem; I just cannot express it very well." The proof of a thought lies in its written expression, and if the expression is nonsense, then probably the thought was nonsense too.

Does that show, however, that there are no non-expressed thoughts? Surely not. Fermat's last theorem, despite having now been proved by Andrew Wiles, remained without a proof for decades. Did Fermat actually have the proof, though he never wrote it down? We shall never know. But he might have done.

Many of us know that we enjoyed a performance at a theatre even if we never told anyone we were even there. We could have said so. But if we did not, and if no friends were there to see us grinning inanely from time to time, no one might ever know. Even if our friends had been with us, they might have thought we had indigestion. We might even have cried with happiness. Unless we explain ourselves, no one will never know we are happy.

And would it make sense for us to say, "I think I am really enjoying this play. But I could be wrong. Perhaps I dislike it intensely"? As Ryle says, this is not a matter of watching the play, and then watching ourselves intently on some inner stage to see if there is some enjoyment there. It is a matter of watching the play in an enjoying sort of way. But that enjoyment, though often expressed in behaviour or in language, may remain wholly unexpressed and unobserved and yet make all the difference to our view of the play.

So there are forms of knowledge that may have no linguistic or behavioural expression. The test of whether it is knowledge will be some public expression – obviously, for that is what a "test" is, publicly observable evidence. But the introspectionist claim is precisely that there is some untestable knowledge. And it seems that the only test of that claim is to have some yourself. Such a test will itself fail the test of being publicly observable, since no one else can test whether you have had some untestable knowledge. So it is a paradoxical sort of test; it is a "suck-it-and-see" test, which depends on assuming what is to be proved – that there is untestable knowledge.

The importance of memories

That is not such a strange idea as it may at first seem. Most of our memories, particularly of things that only we have seen, are in practice untestable. We simply have to believe that they are trustworthy. Although Ryle does not believe in introspection, he does believe in retrospection. We may not have special inner access to what we are doing now, but we may know what we did a few moments ago. Ryle says, "The fact that retrospection is autobiographical does not imply that it gives us a Privileged Access to facts of a special status."[1] We know what we did five minutes ago in the same way that anyone else does or could do, Ryle claims. He says that our knowledge of what we did in the past is "of the same kind" as the knowledge anyone else may have of what we did five minutes ago.

Is this so? For it to be true, we have to make the extraordinary assumption that if I had spoken my thoughts out loud, and if there had been anyone there to hear me, and if they remembered what I said, then – and only then – their knowledge of what I did would be of the same kind as my knowledge of it. In fact I did not speak out loud, and there was no one there to hear or remember what I actually did not say, and yet I remember what I thought. I can remember unspoken thoughts when no one else is there. Nobody else can ever do that with my thoughts. Here, then, is a "kind of knowledge" that nobody else could ever have, in principle.

Anyway, what is the point of a test that can never in practice be carried out? It is like saying, "If I were as small as an electron, then I could observe electrons buzzing busily about." In a similar way, if I had been at the Battle of Waterloo, then I could have observed Napoleon looking worried. But I was not there, and I never could be there. Does a purely hypothetical and indeed impossible hypothesis make an actual memory claim more reliable? Not at all.

My memory claims about the past are of the same kind as other people's memory claims about the past – they are both often untestable. Having two or more untestable claims does not strengthen the evidence for anything. For if I cannot trust one person's claims, the situation cannot be helped by trusting the claims of lots of people, none of whose claims we can trust! It would be rather like asking a twelve-year-old student to state the theory of relativity. Just to check what he says, we ask all his classmates to give their version of the theory. That is only going to make things worse. So if we distrust one person's memory claims, it will not help to ask lots of other people what they remember, because we have no good reason for preferring their memory claims. Adding many untrustworthy memory claims together, so that we get them to agree with each other, is not a guarantee of reliability.

The fact is that we just have to trust uncheckable memory claims. Then, if many people make the same sorts of claims, that does increase our general confidence in their claims. If many fallible people agree, that does not make them infallible. But it normally increases our confidence in our own claims if others make very similar claims (even though we know crowds are more subject to illusions than single individuals).

So we just have to accept, for the sake of our own sanity, that memories are in general trustworthy – which means that we have good reason to accept the memory claims of others. Far from other people's memories serving as necessary confirming evidence of our own memories, it is in fact our belief in the reliability of our own memories that gives rise to the thought that other people's memories are in general reliable too. That thought is then confirmed by our agreeing about the same things, when those things have been publicly observable. But if we have memories about things that nobody else observed, we are still justified in thinking them reliable, other things being equal. Ryle's preference for retrospection over introspection does not work, because many retrospections are about introspections, and both rely on the untestable but wholly reasonable claim that our memories are reliable in general.

What goes for memories goes for inner experiences in general. Some non-sensory untestable knowledge turns out to be essential for human knowledge in general, and such knowledge can and does influence behaviour. Self-knowledge, obtained through introspection, can cause major changes in behaviour and can be of decisive moral importance for a human life. We do well to take the advice of others when assessing our own characters. But we would do very badly to take their advice as the only or last word on what we are and know. Our behaviour is a good clue to what kind of people we are. Yet our unspoken thoughts and feelings should often modify judgments based purely on behaviour in important ways. In a perfect world, we might perhaps express our thoughts and feelings in an uninhibited and open way. In the world as it is, only a very silly or a very saintly (or possibly a very rich) person would do so.

What is most important about a human life is the unique quality of experience a person has and the unique moral choices that a person makes. A person's life is normally the result of a whole series of unique perspectives and choices about what to attend to, what to do, and how to do it, and of a complex of evaluations and feelings in regard to the varied situations that person has encountered and responded to. Those responses are unknowable in many respects by anyone else, and even if they sometimes remain unrecognized to the agent concerned, that agent has an access to them that no one else could have.

The ability to know oneself fully and to direct one's own actions freely to a personally chosen goal in positive cooperation with others is what defines a fully human life. That ability is rarely exercised to any great extent, and it remains for most of us a distant ideal rather than an actual achievement. Ryle is importantly right in drawing attention to the importance of behaviour and of conscious personal interactions with others in human life. He is right to oppose the thought – whether or not Descartes believed it – that human minds are isolated private and ethereal worlds where invisible levers are pulled to make bodies move. But he tends to minimize or, at his worst, to deny that which makes human behaviour and relationship personal – the inner experience and feeling that is what is expressed and shared in personal behaviour and social relationship, and the inner choices and motives that are only partly manifest in outward actions. Human life carries with it the possibility of a fundamental option for the good. That option is often deeply hidden by the ambiguities of our lives. But it may be what defines us as fully human beings.

Chapter Fourteen

The idealist view of life

So I propose philosophical idealism as the most adequate, consistent, and plausible metaphysical view of reality. It carries with it a theory of human persons as experientially unique, morally free, and fully embodied subjects of experience and action, living in an interpersonal world of similar beings – a community of social and self-realizing conscious agents. Idealism is not to be accepted because it is comforting or wish-fulfilling. It is to be accepted because it makes a reasoned claim to be the most intellectually adequate view of reality and of human personhood that human thought has devised.

Of course any philosophical view will remain contested and less than overwhelmingly convincing. This is, after all, philosophy and not chemistry. But we can scarcely escape having some such view, and idealism will always continue to be one of the most intellectually impressive high-points among human attempts to achieve real insight into the nature of the complex and mysterious reality of which we humans are part.

The point of this discussion has been to emphasize that we all have privileged, though not infallible or complete, access to our own inner lives, our thoughts, memories, feelings, and intentions. This fact gives us very important information about the world – namely, that conscious experiences and intentional actions are real, not reducible to material and publicly observable facts, and morally crucial for the way we live.

Materialists, however, have a very different view. They would in general say that conscious experiences, if they exist, are by-products of material processes, so thinking and feeling does not give any special or privileged access to reality. Reality is accessed through scientific (and materialist) theories. Yet for materialists such theories are a by-product, and an unforeseen one at that, of blind laws of nature. So, on a materialist theory, we would not expect that our theories (including the theory of materialism) are particularly reliable or informative vehicles of information about the world.

Materialism gives abstract theory priority over concrete experience, while at the same time it undermines the reliability of the reason and understanding that provides us with our abstract theories. That is like saying that we should trust reason even when what it tells us is that reason is untrustworthy. Something seems to be wrong somewhere.

The idealist resolution of this paradoxical situation is to say that our thoughts, feelings, and perceptions do give us access to reality. They suggest that reality itself may be founded not on blind chance or unconscious necessity, but on some form of purposive consciousness.

Materialists will probably protest that consciousness is a very late evolutionary development, requiring complex brains for its existence. But we need to distinguish the embodied consciousness of beings that exist in a common space-time manifold from a possible non-embodied consciousness that expresses itself in, or forms the causal basis of, the whole space-time manifold itself. The former types of consciousness do come into being as the result of a long process of evolutionary development, and they have a strong causal and epistemic dependence upon their physical environment. The latter type of consciousness does not come into being at all. The physical world depends for its very existence upon the primordial consciousness and perhaps expresses the inner nature of that consciousness, as it brings into being dependent consciousnesses which can share relationships with it.

Why should we think that there is such a primordial consciousness? The strongest form of idealism, that of Bishop Berkeley for instance, would say that only minds are fully real, and there cannot be material things that are not contents of some consciousness. Also the only sort of causal power we directly experience is our own intentional action, which brings things about for a reason. The idea of "material causality" or, more exactly, regularity of succession, is by contrast a relatively abstract notion. On this strong idealist view, the ultimate reality has to be mind, and ultimate causality has to be intentional agency.

Weaker versions of idealism would insist that value (the positive evaluation of personal experiences) and purpose (the effort to bring about future states) are elements of reality that are not analysable in purely material terms. Therefore, mind must at least be a fundamental component of what there is, and if there is some ultimate explanation for the existence of the universe, it must include a mind-like element. Personal explanation (explaining something by saying that it is chosen for a good reason) must be part of the explanation of why the cosmos exists as it does. And it implies that alleged experience of a non-embodied mind, known in and through material appearances, is a real possibility that may be veridical and could provide confirming evidence of the existence of such a mind.

If we give great importance and value to the inner personal lives of human beings, and if we find the distinctiveness of human life to lie largely in the ability to choose goodness for its own sake, then we are committing ourselves to a view of reality that affirms the reality and value of conscious experience and moral goodness. This is opposed to any hard-line materialism that denies the existence or importance of consciousness, and it is opposed to any relativist view of ethics that maintains that the good is whatever certain people happen to prefer. There are real values and they lie in conscious states or actions. Since such values are objective, they suggest the existence of an objective non-human consciousness in which they can be found.

We may also feel that two very different sorts of reality, the material cosmos and the existence of free conscious and intelligent agents, need to be integrated within a coherent and plausible metaphysical framework. The materialist thesis that inner experience and purpose just happen to originate by chance and have no lasting significance does not seem very plausible. Consciousness and purpose simply become inexplicable add-ons to the physical process, and for a tough-minded materialist they may even be quite illusory.

An idealist framework will explain the physical cosmos as existing in order to permit beings who have personal experiences and purposes to share a common environment in which they can learn, develop, and act. But this "in order to" introduces purpose into the basic structure of the physical cosmos, and that introduction suggests that the basic structure of the physical cosmos is mind-like in important respects.

Further, the apparent intelligibility of the world suggests that there are good reasons for why things are as they are; that events do not happen solely by chance. Even the laws of nature exist for a reason, and the best reason is that they exist for the sake of desirable goals which the universe may realize. We are then thinking of a primordial mind that can envisage and evaluate possible goals and bring them about intentionally. That is the heart of the idealist case.

Many idealists would call this primordial consciousness "God". But others find it better to avoid the word "God", because of the many different, and often silly, things that it might mean to them. Idealists do not mean to speak of a person, probably male, who lives outside the universe and interferes in it from time to time, in completely unpredictable ways. They believe that the ultimate nature of reality is more like consciousness than either blind necessity or pure chance. It is a consciousness very unlike human embodied consciousness. It is an independent and generative consciousness, not a dependent and largely receptive one. It contains as part of its substance something like a set of ideal possibilities, which perhaps necessarily express themselves in varied forms of finite material being. Its nature is known by human beings, if it is, as all other minds are known, by seeing the temporal processes of the phenomenal world as expressions of a largely hidden mental content.

For idealists like Hegel, primordial mind is not some being apart from the physical universe. It is the inner nature of the universe itself. It does not conjure up the universe out of nothing by some arbitrary act of will. It realizes its own necessary nature in a progressive process of temporal unfolding. It is not a person who chooses to create suffering and tragedy just because it wants to, when it could easily have chosen otherwise. Suffering and tragedy are parts of its own being, possibilities necessarily inherent in its self-objectification. Nevertheless, it could be said to have a moral goal or purpose – as a rational consciousness, it "aims at" the realization of many sorts of valuable states for their own sake. And it may actualize freedom and mutuality as well as necessity and a monopoly of causal power. That is, the cosmos it objectifies may generate many personal agencies capable of moral choice and social relationship, with a degree of autonomous causal power. Indeed in this cosmos it seems to do precisely that.

Presumably such a mind will have knowledge of whatever becomes actual in the cosmos. Most idealists suppose that while it will retain complete knowledge of all that has ever existed, within its own cosmic experience it will mitigate destructive and painful experiences by subordinating them to and placing them in a wider context of creative and valuable experiences. Within that context they may be seen as inevitable, or at least as non-removable, parts of an emergent cosmos in which societies of creatively and morally free finite agents exist. In this way it will fulfil the goal of its own self-realization.

Idealism is certainly a "grand metaphysical theory", and as such it is the main philosophical competitor with materialism. And both idealism and materialism are competitors with a Rylean or Wittgensteinian disinterestedness in such grand metaphysical systems.

Philosophy and metaphysics

I suspect that Ryle would say, in response to all this, that if we are thinking about the concept of mind, and we get too far away from the ordinary language that we use about human minds and the everyday contexts in which we use that language, our concepts will no longer have any purchase on reality. They will be like cog wheels spinning energetically on their own without connecting to any useful mechanism. We should look at the informal logic of mental-conduct concepts as they are actually used, and not try to invent purely hypothetical and untestable theories about how they might be used in totally different, probably inconceivable, circumstances. Talk of "ultimate reality" is like talk of "ultimate Platonic trousers": all very well in theory but not very good for covering your legs.

Unfortunately, once philosophers had eliminated the great classical philosophical systems as based on grammatical mistakes, and had demonstrated that the language that ordinary people speak is quite in order as it is, as long as ordinary people do not ask silly questions about it, there was nothing left for philosophers to do. It is rather ironic that Ryle, as a great philosophy teacher, was able to place most of his pupils (including me) in university jobs as professional philosophers, where they were paid to proclaim that there was no such profession as philosophy.

I had to teach a course in moral philosophy in the 1960s (I will not say where), and I recall the widespread philosophical view that there was no point in asking moral philosophers about difficult ethical issues, since their opinion was no better than anyone else's. Moral philosophers could write long monographs about how people use words like "good" or "right", but they were not qualified to express any moral opinions. Looking around at some of my colleagues, I thought that perhaps this was a very good thing.

In a similar way, metaphysics was a form of armchair palaeontology – the study of fossilized philosophical systems that were now all extinct. If asked what the nature of reality was, philosophers would reply, "It all depends on what you mean by real," and then patiently explain that real hair consisted in not wearing a wig or that real antiques were not new things that had been shot full of holes to look like ancient woodworm. If unwise undergraduates persisted in saying that they were seeking for what things were made of, they would be told that some things were made of wood, some of plastic, and some had not been made at all. It is not surprising that philosophy classes became progressively less well attended. Ancient philosophers like David Hume had played backgammon because philosophy was too difficult. Modern philosophers played backgammon because philosophy was too easy and consisted mostly in getting people to stop asking philosophical questions – which they could do best by not going to philosophy lectures.

That, however, is no longer the case. Partly because physicists have stepped in where philosophers refused to tread, and partly because medical practice and new technology generated a new range of ethical problems that do need some expertise to address, philosophy has started to get interested in the large traditional metaphysical and ethical issues again. "What is the real?" and "What is the good?" are no longer naive questions. People really want to know if the natural sciences are the only ways of finding out the truth, and if there is any way of reasonably resolving the ethical dilemmas that modern medicine puts before us.

Imagining minds

Materialism battles with idealism – and scientists line up on both sides. Utilitarianism battles with moral absolutism – and both politicians and doctors find themselves on opposing sides here too.

Any objective observer would say that we are in a situation where many diverse and competing views can be reasonably defended. I am not persuaded that ordinary linguistic usage should be the final test of whether we are talking sense or making sense of human existence. If anything, I tend to think that ordinary linguistic usages are liable to be quite misleading, to express prejudices and half-digested philosophical theories whose origin has been forgotten.

I certainly think that if we are considering the concept of mind, we should not limit ourselves to the sorts of minds we know best – human minds. We should explore the possibility of other kinds of minds, by imaginative extrapolation. The idea of a cosmic mind is a particularly interesting one, because it takes the notions of knowledge, feeling, and power to the highest degree we can think of. If we grant the existence of consciousness and objective value, we can try to conceive a consciousness of supreme value, knowledge, feeling, and power, and try to say what in general it would be like. That is indeed what many writers of science fiction do – and they often describe possible realities that some philosophers cannot imagine. Perhaps, as Tom Stoppard once said, "There are more things in my philosophy than are dreamed of in reality." Or perhaps such dreams give a hint of what reality might really be like.

The cosmic mind may not have all these properties to the highest possible degree, and, if not, it should perhaps try harder. Anyhow, idealist views are not committed to the "highest degree of mind" view, pleasing though that might be. What they are committed to is that the reality underlying sensory appearances is more like a conscious and purposive cause of the phenomenal cosmos than it is like unconscious globs of unintelligent stuff (or maybe one super-glob of super-stupidity) from which the cosmos emerges without purpose or design. Or if purpose and design remind you too much of God, we might say that an idealist cosmos would at least exist for a reason, and it would exhibit an intelligible order.

If an idealist philosophy is adopted, this will have implications for the way human persons see themselves in relation to the cosmos of which they are parts. Most basically, they will find in their own inner lives of apprehension, feeling, and intention, a resonance or unity with the inner reality of the cosmos. Human consciousness will not be a freak, transient accident in a basically lifeless and indifferent universe. It will have a place in the self-realization of cosmic mind. The world revealed to us in sensory experience will be seen as an expression of cosmic mind – sometimes terrifying and dangerous, sometimes beautiful and awe-inspiring, but always expressive of a deep consciousness beyond the veil of the senses. The world may be "read" as an interaction with cosmic mind, somewhat as other human bodies are read as expressions of conscious feelings and aims. Humans will be fundamentally "at home" in the universe; not alien intrusions into a realm of blind laws, but integral parts of a self-expressive process oriented toward the realization of objective personal values.

Within such a world view, the arts can be seen as participations in the creativity of the cosmos, in a power beyond the finite self that yet works through and can heighten the insights and skills of artistic endeavour. Great works of art, music, and literature will be disclosive of what George Steiner calls "real presence", communications of transcendent mind as perceived by the immanent and embodied minds of human beings.

Science will be seen as the discovery of a real intelligible order in the natural world, an order with a beauty and rationality that can be partly captured by mathematical exploration. The ancient Greeks were right – mathematics is the key to the order of the universe. For some peculiar reason, they did not devote much time to testing their mathematical theories by experimental observation, insisting that their maths was right without looking to see. But they did see what modern science has often failed to see, that a rational universe will be one in which the laws of nature will themselves have a reason. The only plausible candidate for such a reason is not the existence of a further set of hyper-laws. It is that for the sake of which all laws exist, the efficient realization of intrinsic values.

Morality will be a response to an objective moral ideal and goal for the cosmos itself, a goal which humans can play a part in realizing. It will not be the construction of compromise rules which can mediate between opposing social interests. The good life will be a life lived for the sake of good, both in oneself and in society. It will be part of the realization of distinctive values which forms the ultimate reason for the existence of the cosmos. Devotion to the good for its own sake will thus also be devotion to that ultimate mind by which the good is conceived and in which it is progressively realized. This makes possible that "intellectual love of God", of the source and completion of the good, which was the centre of Spinoza's philosophy.

Human history will not only be a story of the interactions of human persons as they formulate cultural ideals and seek to make a distinctive contribution to the human world. It will also be an expression of the self-realization of transcendent mind, as it generates many diverse embodied minds, allows them creative and moral freedom, interacts with them as they impede or realize its purposes, and leads them through objectification and alienation toward a wider goal of a global society of societies. Hegel developed most fully this view of what he saw as the planetary history of Absolute Spirit. We may view his specific analyses and predictions with some scepticism. Karl Marx even found it necessary to stand Hegel on his head and get rid of a higher consciousness altogether, though he did not do any better himself. But that should not put us off the thought that in some way human relationships may also be the vehicles of the expression of the inner nature of the cosmos as it moves toward a moral goal that is inherent in its own inner being.

Cosmic optimism

Idealists tend to be optimistic about the universe, thinking that value will be progressively realized in it. Even then, however, they usually accept that the universe will come to an end in a few billion years or so. Their optimism is not unqualified. Indeed some of them go around looking rather gloomy, and saying, "It may seem good now, but mark my words, in a few billion years this will all be gone." The super-optimists, however, refuse to accept this depressing thought. Bolstered by some of the weirder extremes of cosmology and artificial intelligence research, they think that human beings will manage to download themselves into super-computers and move off into inter-galactic space, as our sun runs out of steam (more precisely, out of heat).

By the time our universe runs down, they will then have become even cleverer, and will be able to travel through a black hole into a brand new universe. So they can keep going forever, moving from one universe to another, intelligences of immense knowledge and power, living in the huge seeming emptiness between the galaxies, hidden from all the relatively minute intelligences slowly emerging in those universes.

If this is so, then in our universe today there are probably huge numbers of super-intelligences living in outer space, and having super-committee-meetings about how they might guide the affairs of the little primitive carbon-based life forms emerging in their local universe. Religions may sometimes seem weird, but they have nothing on some modern cosmological speculations. A favourite among such speculations as I write is the many-worlds or multiverse theory. It holds that every possible universe exists, the whole set of universes forming a super-universe or multiverse.

It is not often realized that on this theory, every possible array of gods, goddesses, devils, and angels will exist somewhere in some universe. So every possible religion and philosophy will be true, but all in different universes. We can correctly believe in God in one universe and correctly be an atheist in another. We can even be parts of God in some universes and parts of Lucifer in others. The possibilities are endless. Even materialist atheism can be true in some universes, where no super-intelligences ever visit, and only the illusion of consciousness exists (I am not sure what that would feel like or who would be having the illusion, but now we've got the story going, let's run with it as far as possible).

Speculative science has thus far outstripped idealism in its classical forms. But the surprising thing is that these possibilities, though they are indeed fantastic, seem to be not only logically possible, but physically possible. Common-sense philosophy can be seen to be merely a restriction on human imagination. Perhaps common-sense philosophers should stay in more and read more science fiction. If they do that, they will soon find themselves asking, "Which universe do I actually live in?" And I do not think the answer is at all clear.

Of course that is the main reason for being a common-sense philosopher. We cannot make our minds up between all the possible universes we might be living in, and so we drop the subject and just respond to particular problems as and when they come up.

On making ultimate metaphysical decisions

Idealists, like everyone else, can distinguish between speculation and real existential decisions – decisions which make a real, practical, important difference to the way we live. The question of whether our descendants might one day decant themselves into a super-computer and disappear down a black hole is purely speculative. It opens the mind to the possibility of the continued existence of intelligent life even after this universe has run down and given up the ghost (or all its ghosts). But it is not something we should count on or look forward to in the next decade or so.

However, our answer to the question of whether this cosmos has an objective moral goal which we can play a part in actualizing might make a difference to how we see our lives and to how we live. If we see human lives as lived in a dialectical or ambiguous relationship to the goals of cosmic mind, as alienated by hatred, greed, and ambition and yet haunted by the ideal of a more creative and compassionate global community, that might make us see ourselves and other persons in a new light. We might see persons as "called" to a distinctive way of life, which is to be achieved only by overcoming the attractions of pleasure, power, and indifference that would frustrate such a life. Each person would be both a potential vehicle of expressing a higher consciousness and also a partial obstacle to its expression. In that dialectic of expression and obstruction each person would be part of a continuing interplay between transcendent mind and many socially embodied minds, an interplay which weaves history into the complex patterns it displays.

Whether the pattern of history moves inevitably toward a society on this planet in which values are freely created and shared without restriction is perhaps not as clear as Hegel and Marx both thought. It might be that our world will, despite T. S. Eliot, end with a bang and not with a whimper. Humanity could be a cosmic experiment that is about to fail, and, as *The Hitchhiker's Guide to the Galaxy* predicts, our planet might be removed to make way for a cosmic motorway or for some more successful form of life. Since we cannot be sure, maybe the best we can do is to hope and work for the best and yet prepare for the worst. That way we might at least find, as tourists do when they contemplate the weather while on holiday in England, that we will be very pleased that things did not turn out to be quite as bad as they could have been. And that could be part of the recipe for a happy life.

Idealism need not be religious, in the sense of leading to membership of some religious institution. Many idealists regard most religions as a mass of superstitions and legends, with unduly submissive attitudes toward various holy books, all of which contradict one another. But idealism may be sympathetic to some kinds of religion or spirituality, as attempted human responses to transcendent mind, intended to achieve liberation from self-centred egoism and to evoke a sense of union with or positive relation to a reality of wisdom, compassion, and bliss.

For some people, idealism is best seen as an abstract intellectual attempt by weak and partly corrupted human reason to approach a truth that has been independently revealed in a more emotionally accessible way by God – that is, I think, what most Christians think about Hegel. Even if that is so, idealism will remain an intriguing testimony to a residual sense of the ontological primacy of mind, of the reality of the soul and of God. For others, the reverse will be true, and various religions may be symbolic and pictorial ways of approaching the philosophical truth of idealism – that is what Hegel thought about most Christians.

Whatever view you take about that, idealism seems to me the most coherent, comprehensive, integrative, and plausible conceptual scheme for understanding the world of which we are parts. As a basic metaphysical scheme, it does not need and cannot have "evidence", in the sense of publicly observable experimental demonstration. Like any ambitiously large-scale philosophy, it is based on reasons drawn from a wide range of data. Different philosophies stress different aspects of these data as of primary importance, and idealism stresses the irreducibility and importance of consciousness, reason, and morality.

There are alternative metaphysical schemes. For some, the conceptual disentangling of mind from the context of its human embodiment in brain, body, and society is a step too far, and may seem like the invention of a fantastic fiction. They will not be able to see the life of the human mind as one of response to transcendent mind through art, science, morality, and quotidian experience. It will still be possible, however, to see the life of the mind as one of creative and empathetic interaction with other embodied minds, and to find the best kind of human life to be the common pursuit of the good and the beautiful, even in a world plagued by violence and injustice and destined to end in universal cosmic death. Some would hold that human life becomes more precious by recognition of its sheer fortuitousness, its brevity, and its inevitable end.

While not sharing that view myself, I recognize in it a tragic nobility, and I feel that a life committed to such a pursuit would be a life well worth living. Maybe it is really all one can have. Yet it would not be unreasonable to hope for more. Some of us think we have more, not particularly in visions or peculiar and overwhelming "religious experiences", but in a general confirmation throughout many forms of personal experience of a sense of transcendent presence that speaks of a mind other and greater than ours or of what William Arnold called "an enduring Power, not ourselves, which makes for righteousness". I doubt if this is a matter that philosophy alone can resolve, although philosophical reflection may help to make clearer the different presuppositions it is reasonable to adopt and some of the logical consequences of adopting them.

Chapter Fifteen

Can we still speak of the soul?

I conclude the book with some references to the views of Plato, Aristotle, Descartes, and the Bible. I draw attention to particular affinities that exist between their views and those expressed here. Idealism is a philosophy, not a religion, but it has an elective affinity with some religious views insofar as they are genuinely humanistic, and it shares with them an aversion to materialism, especially in its reductive or eliminative forms. Insofar as religions have a philosophical basis, it will usually be a form of idealism. Insofar as idealists seek ritual, moral, and communal expression for their views, they may find it in some form of religion.

However that may be, I will conclude with a final homage to and divergence from Gilbert Ryle. I should say that he would agree with the first of the following sentences, and probably remain baffled by the second: there is no ghost, and there is no machine. There is only the reality of mind, and its expression and appearance in the dynamic and developing forms of an open and emergent material universe.

I have mentioned the soul once or twice in previous chapters, though I have generally preferred to talk about the human person or the mind. Yet of course I have been speaking throughout of what has been traditionally thought of as the human soul, and in this last chapter I will connect what I have said with some traditional philosophical and religious views.

We do not speak much of the soul these days, though the ancient Greek word for soul – *psyche* – can be translated as "mind". Perhaps *psyche* is rather broader in reference, since it can be used to refer to all living things rather than just to mind. But it does not have to refer to something higher than minds and detachable from them. The soul is nevertheless often thought of as a distinct spiritual substance which is added to the body at some early stage of life, and which departs at death to continue its existence in its own immaterial way. Plato did seem to speak of the soul in that way, saying in some dialogues that all souls were destined to return to their true homes in the stars, once they had escaped their bondage to physical bodies. One problem with this view is that it is hard to see what souls will do all day if they have no bodies. Perhaps they just twinkle or spend their time doing arithmetic in their heads – except of course they have no heads. That is not something that most of us would look forward to with keen anticipation.

But being Plato, he did not always think that, and he had a much more positive view of physical bodies in the *Timaeus*, where he even spoke of the physical cosmos as a "visible god", and of souls as finding visible and sometimes beautiful expression within the cosmos.

Plato divided the soul into three parts, but he did so largely in order to make a neat and tidy comparison between the individual and society. In *The Republic* he divides the classes of society into three – the rulers, the guardians, and the rest. The rulers, after long training, could tell what the best kind of society would be. The guardians were the executive power, an armed guard who could defend the state and enforce the decisions of the rulers. The rest carried on trade and did other sorts of menial and unworthy but necessary things. Plato wished to argue that justice ruled when all these parts of society were content with their proper place in the social order.

When he came to speak of justice in the individual soul, he similarly tried to speak of it as a sort of internal order. Reason should rule. There should be a part for enforcing rational decisions. We might call this "the will", which puts decisions into effect. But Plato called it *thumos*, a "spirited" element, whose defining virtue is courage and a sense of honour or righteous indignation. The third element is desire. In the well-ordered soul, honour would execute the decisions of reason, and control desire. In a badly ordered soul, desire, and passionate action might overwhelm reason.

This threefold Platonic division is not quite that of Ryle's pet hate – the division of mind into thought, will, and feeling, three separate faculties each doing their own job. But it is pretty close. There is a contemplative faculty, an executive faculty, and a faculty closely bound up with bodily needs, wants, and feelings. This, Ryle says, is "such a welter of confusions and false inferences that it is best to give up any attempt to re-fashion it".[1]

Ryle's point is that there are so many different sorts of mental activity that it is pointless to try to divide them up into a specific number of ways of thinking, as though there was a little committee inside the brain which divides mental jobs up rather neatly between its members. It is only fair to recall, however, that Plato is not seeking to give a systematic analysis of mind. What he basically wants to say is that in the just soul the passions and desires should be ordered to good ends by reason, and that to order often unruly desires some fairly aggressive and resolute discipline is called for. The inner mental disciplinarian is *thumos*, which we might call resolution or determination, the guardian and overseer of desire. It is not unlike Nietzsche's "will to power". If it is not controlled by reason, it will seek vitality and ambition for their own sakes. But when controlled by reason, it will order desires toward the cultivation of personal excellence and the realization of that which is good and beautiful.

We need not speak of "three parts of the soul". We could simply say that we have bodily appetites, but we are capable of reflecting on what is fully good and worthwhile, and we can discipline our appetites to aim habitually and by nature at such things. A good human life requires desires to be controlled effectively by dispassionate understanding and an iron will. Plato's metaphorical talk of the faculties of the soul makes this point very well. It is after all true that human minds think abstractly and understand, feel pleasure and pain and many diverse subjective responses to what impacts on human bodies, and are able (or at least think they are able) to act to control their bodies and environments to some extent. These are the main elements appealed to in forms of personal explanation. So even if Plato's terminology differs somewhat from ours, it alludes to the main basic elements that characterize human mentality, and it clearly places an emphasis on the importance of moral action (action for the sake of good) in human life. It also brings out the importance of having a view of human nature that can make sense of moral action in a universe like this. To have a picture of the nature of morality is already to have a picture of human nature. What philosophy does is try to make that picture explicit.

Aristotle on the soul

Despite the immense importance of Plato in the history of Western philosophy, it was Aristotle who formulated the most influential Western definition of the soul, when he said that it was the "form" (*eidos*) of the body. A form is the essential nature of something, that which makes it what it is and not another thing. All things, for Aristotle as for Plato, incarnate forms; they have essential or proper natures. But organic forms, the natures of organisms, have a special role as defining what it is a developing organism is "aiming at" or tending by nature to be. Thus the form of a human embryo is to be a specific human adult, with the capacities and dispositions of that fully grown organism. Or the form of an acorn is the fully grown oak tree.

Each organic form has a set of specific capacities that are proper to it. For Aristotle, vegetative forms have the capacity for growth and reproduction. More complex animal forms have the capacity for movement and sentience. Human, intelligent forms have the capacity for abstract thought and responsible action. Thus in speaking of forms we are speaking of sets of capacities proper to organisms of a specific kind. When we say that the soul, more properly the intellectual soul, or the mind, is the form of a human body, we mean these sets of capacities are proper to human beings as such.

Aristotle's doctrine of the soul or mind is thus that some intellectual and moral capacities and propensities are distinctive of and proper to organisms that are members of the human species. To say what the human soul is is to say what the distinctive, proper capacities of human beings are. I believe that Gilbert Ryle would accept this view, with one important and decisive proviso. All essentialist and teleological elements must be removed from the idea of a "form".

The rise of modern science involved a rejection of the idea that substances have essential natures, which they are "meant" to embody. Rather, the natural world is a continuum of many different properties, capacities, and forces. One shades into another without any clear demarcation line, and there are many blurred edges and overlaps. As Wittgenstein put it, there are many family resemblances between things and processes, but there need be no central defining characteristic that makes a thing what it is.

Evolution is often interpreted in this way, leading to views that humans are not sharply distinguished from higher primates, and that, as a class, they have no necessary and sufficient defining characteristics. Some humans have no intelligence, and some intelligences are not human. Humans are beings that resemble each other (and also other animals) in varying ways and to varying degrees, like different members of a family. Therefore (it is sometimes said) humans have, as such, no peculiar moral value or worth.

In the same way, the idea of final causality was widely rejected in the seventeenth century. Organisms do not "aim at" some ideal state, for the sake of which they exist. They usually pass through a cycle of growth and decay, without aim or purpose, just happening to reproduce on the way. Therefore (it is sometimes said) there is no particular sort of thing that humans ought to be or no sort of life that humans are meant by nature to live.

I think Aquinas was right in suggesting that the Aristotelian view only made sense based on the supposition that there is some kind of cosmic mind which contains the ideal forms that define what things properly are in their fullest development or what the innate goals of their existence are. Idealists will naturally have no problem with such a view, and it fits well with the belief that intellectual understanding, creative freedom, and interpersonal empathy are objective goals of the cosmic process. It is not the human species, as such, that is of special value. Any being capable of understanding, freedom, and empathy has special moral worth – just the "faculties" of thought, will, and feeling so derided by Ryle. For this reason, "humanism" is not the most appropriate term for that concentration on personal flourishing that was one of the theoretical marks of the European Enlightenment. It would be better to speak of personalism, the postulation of intelligible thought, creative will, and empathetic feeling as intrinsic moral goods, to be protected and maximized wherever they occur.

I think it makes good sense to say that any beings with such capacities are of distinctive worth and should be respected as such. It also makes sense to say that human beings are such beings or are parts or offspring of such societies of beings, and so incarnate a specific character or form which is morally important. To sustain, enhance, and cherish such capacities, and to oppose all that frustrates them, both in oneself and in others, as far as is possible, is a distinctive moral goal for human lives.

What modern science opposes is answering questions about the natures of things with merely verbal definitions. What is required is experimentation, observation, and testable predictions. Natural science is not concerned with the aims natural things might have, but with the regular processes by which things change. But that does not mean that there are no goals in nature or that those goals cannot be defined in terms of distinctive capacities. Values and purposes have not been the concern of the natural sciences for some centuries. But the exclusion of the personal from the realm of natural science does not exclude it from reality. It is for philosophical reflection to define what worthwhile purposes may be, using all the available data provided by the natural sciences, but adding data from the rich historical records of human personal and moral experience, and making the most comprehensive personal evaluation of all this data.

Cartesian dualism and beyond

When the Aristotelian philosophy was replaced by the more mechanistic approach of classical science, it became difficult for philosophers to integrate personal values and purposes into the increasingly influential world view of natural science. Cartesian dualism was one symptom of this difficulty, separating mental substance from material substance in such a way that it was difficult to see how one could interact with the other. As I have emphasized, Descartes believed in such integration, but did not find a plausible way of formulating it. It was to take the discovery of evolution to do so, with the picture it opened up of a gradually more complex and emergent process leading to the development of mind as an increasingly autonomous inner aspect of matter.

A Cartesian hangover from Aristotle was the notion of substance, an enduring substratum that could contain various changing properties. For many philosophers, this was slowly replaced by the idea of process, of a flowing succession of properties, located in space and time. The idea of substance could be retained as the idea of a core bundle of properties that could change more or less gradually over time. The idea of strict numerical identity was replaced by the idea of a succession of properties, "identity" being largely a matter of degree and convenience. A tree generated from the pruned stump of a prior tree could be called the same tree or not, almost at will.

In modern science, questions of identity are often treated as matters for conventional decision, upon which nothing much turns. With personal and mental lives, however, the idea of identity becomes morally important. It matters to me whether tomorrow I will remember the plans I made yesterday and be able to continue them or whether I will take over the plans of someone else and pass them on to another person in turn. "This is just what I planned to do" is very different from "This is what he (someone otherwise just like me) would have wanted me to do."

Ryle notwithstanding, it is the chain of privately accessible experiences and actions, thoughts and intentions, that makes the difference. When one and only one person can have such private access, then I could reasonably say that the same personal subject of experience and action continues to exist. The sense of being one and the same continuing subject of many experiences and acts is important to a person. That, I think, is what Descartes meant by a mental substance. For that reason, there is little or no substantial difference between being a mental substance and being a process of privately accessible, temporally flowing events and acts. That is just what being a mental substance is.

Descartes held that the mental substance could exist without the physical substance of the body. But he did not hold that it should, that it did or that it would be a full and proper person if it did. In this, too, he is surely correct. There can, logically, be a succession of thoughts and feelings without any physical body or brain or universe. Perhaps they would be thoughts and feelings about a universe in which we used to have a body and a brain. Perhaps disembodied minds would be condemned to repeat their past embodied experiences over and over again.

On the other hand, perhaps chains of mental acts could find new forms of embodiment in different environments. When Plato speaks of the soul's journey of a thousand years between earthly births, he is speaking as if there are bodies of some sort, receiving experiences from some form of environment, good or bad. And his story is relatable without obvious contradiction. Perhaps it is in some such world, unfathomably far in our future and from this space-time complex, that minds once embodied here could find a fulfilment rare and strange, where fully shared understanding, cooperative creativity, and mutually reinforcing happiness could ameliorate and transfigure all the conflicts and sufferings of our previous lives. And yet those past lives would have been the way of bringing us to our final goal, a way that we were partly thrown into and partly chose, but which was always destined for final good, and which, if we saw it whole, we would embrace with repentance and with joy.

That is the dream of idealism. But is it true? It must be plainly said that there is no proof. Yet it is more than an idle wish. It is rooted in the firm belief that mind is the ultimate nature of being, and that intelligent mind aims, as far as it can, at goodness, at what is worthwhile for its own sake. This dream is what mind would realize if it could, if it were at all possible. It does seem possible, since it contains no contradiction. Dare we then hope for it?

What we should commit ourselves to is the importance of freedom, of moral commitment, of nobility of character, of intellectual and moral virtue, of personal fulfilment and flourishing for all. With this goes a sense of the importance of mind or personhood, of a moral intelligence embedded in an emergent physical world. One might be agnostic about questions concerning an objective spiritual basis of reality. I fully understand that. But moral action requires passionate commitment, not based on evidence (in the sense of demonstration beyond reasonable doubt or even probabilistic judgment), but consonant with one's most basic world view.

That world view may remain largely implicit and obscure, even to oneself. Yet if one commits to the importance of morality, this is an implicit commitment to the importance of mind, if morality is not to be fundamentally irrational. It is entirely reasonable to root these commitments in a basic ontological option for the rationality and goodness (moral orderedness) of being. Then we can root our morality in a response to what is most fully real, what is possible of fuller realization, and what will satisfy personal striving for fulfilment in many diverse and unique historically situated vocations. This is faith – trust that reality is what it seems to us in our highest moments of insight to be. It is validated by practice and by the experience of a life sustained by love.

The soul and immortality

Some people speak of belief in immortality as based on a desire to find some supernatural sanction for moral conduct. If there is a supernatural power that will reward goodness and punish badness, this adds force to moral motivation. But that is to my mind an unduly negative way of putting things. Belief in immortality is primarily based on belief that the ultimate character of reality is mind. This builds consciousness, value, and purpose into the universe in a fundamental way, and prevents one from seeing existence as pure chance, accident or unforeseen happenstance. It roots moral action in a perception of objective purposes of value which it is a human responsibility to further. It gives rise to a presumption that such goals will be achieved if it is possible to achieve them. The point is not that I will be punished or rewarded for my acts. The point is that moral action will not be in vain. My turning away from justice and compassion will lead to my inhabiting a world of injustice, violence, conflict, and hatred. My growth toward greater justice and love will lead to my living in a world of friendship, cooperation, and universal empathy.

In the world as we see it, it is in very general terms true that heroic moral acts lead to a happier and more flourishing society, and that violence breeds its own destruction. But this is only true in general. In millions of particular cases, the innocent perish and the evil flourish. Moral action seems ineffective, and personal sacrifice is in vain. It is not a selfish desire to continue to exist that leads to belief in immortality. It is the impact of the thought that goodness will not triumph, and that the noblest moral sacrifices will fade into insignificance in an indifferent universe.

In a universe in which mind is primary and aims at good, it would contradict the rational structure of the universe if that were the last word. If value and purpose are primary in the universe, then there must be some possibility of rectification of the ills of this life, space for fuller development of our feeble moral efforts, and the possibility of a fuller realization of the value of finite being than seems to be possible in this life. Thus it is deeply rational to hope for a life of the mind beyond the death of this body.

That does not mean that this life becomes less important, while we simply wait for better times hereafter. This life is part of the human pilgrimage, and what is done in it determines what shall become of human lives. In a world corrupted by evil, conflict, and injustice, we have a unique personal part to play in an unfolding scenario of trials encountered and endured, of values envisaged and realized, of tasks undertaken and achieved. Our life is not sound and fury, signifying nothing. It has been like a journey into a far country, from which, chastened and taught by experience, we must at last return. As Plato puts it in Orphic mythology, after our "journey of a thousand years" through the earth, we may shine as stars in the sky. Or, in a Christian version of the same hope, after we have passed through the fires of purification (Mark 9:49 and 1 Corinthians 3:13–15), we may at last shine like the sun in the kingdom of the Father (Matthew 13:43).

This mention of Orphic and Christian symbols may be thought to be introducing religion into a philosophical work. And it may indeed seem that if there is a supreme cosmic mind, it would be rather strange if it disclosed nothing of its nature and purpose in some form of revelation. Nevertheless, this book belongs to philosophy, because it makes no reference to any revealed truths, and its arguments do not depend upon any specific religious teachings. What it does, though, is give many religious interpretations of the human soul a strong rational foundation, suggest the wisdom of at least attending to religious claims for revelation, and support the importance of an understanding of human persons as moral agents whose lives have unique value and a moral purpose that gives them inalienable significance and meaning.

Biblical views of the soul

In a book about the nature of human persons, it would be absurd to overlook religious views entirely. So I will end by saying something about the biblical view of the soul that has been so influential, especially in Western culture. One major problem here is that Plato and Aristotle, or a mixture of the two, have often been more important than what the Bible says. For this reason, there is frequently much confusion about what the Christian or Jewish view of the soul is. The strange truth is that there is, strictly speaking, no biblical, Hebrew or Greek word for "soul", even though the word "soul" is constantly used in English translations of the Bible.

In Hebrew there are three words – *nephesh, neshamah,* and *ruach* – which can each be translated as breath, soul or spirit. None of them seems to denote a thing, substance or entity. They are more like activities or energies. In Genesis 2:7, God formed man "from the dust of the ground", and breathed into his nostrils "the breath of life". Later, in Genesis 7:22, it is reported that, during the great flood everything on dry land in whose nostrils was "the breath of life" died.

The breath of life is common to all breathing animals, so in this sense "the soul" might be taken as that which keeps animals alive and breathing. It is not particularly mental or conscious, but it is some sort of vitality or energy, perhaps something like what the philosopher Henri Bergson called the *élan vital,* life force.

Humans are made from dust and filled by God with vital energy. The first creation story in Genesis 1:26 adds that humans are made in the "image and likeness" of God, having dominion over other life forms. There is much discussion about what exactly this means, but one main interpretation is that humans are entrusted with stewardship of the earth, so that they can act as God does with justice and mercy toward other lives, and stand in the place of God upon this planet.

Some writers have protested that this gives humans too much power, licensing them to do whatever they want with the earth and with other animals. This seems to be against the spirit of the biblical account, however, since all things belong to God, and the role of humans can only be to do God's will, though to do it with a sense of personal responsibility.

For the Genesis stories, humans are special not because they alone have souls, but because, being material and breathing beings, they have a responsibility to order the living things in the world in a just and compassionate way, thereby helping to realize the divine purpose for creation and sharing in the divine work of bringing finite things to the fulfilment for which they were created.

The Hebrew Bible does not show any great interest in a separate spiritual realm apart from this material world. Indeed, for most of the Hebrew Bible, there is no positive view of any life beyond death. The Bible is concerned with realizing justice and compassion in this material world, and humans, as fully material beings – "dust" – have the responsibility to do that.

It is for that reason that when belief in an afterlife became more important, at the time when the very latest passages of the Hebrew Bible were being written, it was thought of in a rather material way. There might be a "resurrection of the body", not just a continuance of disembodied souls. There might be a "new heaven and earth", not a non-physical existence of some sort. We can conclude, then, that the Hebrew (Old Testament) view of the soul is that it is not something that could or should float free of the body. A piece of matter has a soul if it has a sense of responsibility and all that implies – knowledge, freedom, and moral sensibility. Any material entity with those capacities would have a soul. So the possession of a soul is the possession of a set of capacities that entail consciousness, evaluation, and purposive causality (the existence of mind). But those capacities are possessed by a material entity, by dust enlivened by the divine life, not by an immaterial entity that may or may not be embodied in matter.

Nevertheless, there was some idea of an afterlife in early biblical thought. *Sheol* is the place of the dead, like Hades in the Latin tradition. It is not much to be looked forward to, but past persons do seem to reside there – Samuel was called up from *Sheol* by the witch of Endor (1 Samuel 28). There were also angels of various sorts, and some Old Testament characters were said to have ascended to heaven – Enoch, Moses, and Elijah were popular candidates. Apparently there were other realms apart from this earthly one, where past persons could exist in some sense.

Since ordinary physical bodies do not go to *Sheol*, it must be possible for persons to transfer to other sorts of bodies. The soul may not be an immaterial entity, but persons can be embodied in different ways. In later Jewish thought, ideas of a place of punishment (probably temporary) and of paradise developed, presumably as intermediate states before the general resurrection.

In later Christian tradition, this became the doctrine of purgatory or, in the Eastern Orthodox traditions, of the intermediate state, where experiences of various kinds occur to persons who neither exist in their earthly flesh-and-blood bodies, nor in their perfected and glorious resurrection bodies, which will exist only when the whole of heaven and earth and all living things have been renewed.

The whole biblical tradition of course is opposed to materialism. It is idealist, in that it is centred on a knowing, intending, and creating God who is not embodied in any sense. *Ruach*, the breath or spirit of God, is the energizing power of God that shapes creation out of primal chaos (Genesis 1:1–2), and that inspires prophets and heroes. Part of being created "in the image" of God is being able consciously to share in this creative power of God, and so participate in a spiritual and non-material power that has causal influence in the material world.

In the New Testament, *nephesh* is rendered into Greek as *psyche*, and *ruach* as *pneuma*. Again, *psyche* is usually translated into English as "soul", but again it primarily refers to any embodied living animal, anything that "has breath". As Christian thought developed, humans were distinguished as a sub-class of animals that have an "intellectual soul", a specific set of intellectual capacities, especially knowledge, freedom, and moral sense. These capacities were seen as capable of being embodied in different non-flesh-and-blood forms (purgatory or paradise), though it was important that they had been generated and cultured in earthly life. And their final destiny was thought of as a transfigured yet fulfilled form, still individual, still social, still personal, of their first earthly embodiment.

In the key New Testament passage on the resurrection of the dead, Paul distinguishes between the *soma psychikon* and the *soma pneumatikon* (1 Corinthians 15:44). We die, he says, in the former, in bodies filled with the breath of physical living things. But we are resurrected in the latter, in bodies filled with the divine breath or Spirit. They are in some sense bodies, yet they are not the same in kind as ordinary material bodies. They have been transfigured by the divine Spirit, to become knowers and mediators of Spirit, freed from ignorance and selfish desire, free to cooperate with the creative purposes of Spirit. The environment in which they live will be different from this world, free from the laws of transience and decay, and yet the later prophets foresee that this world will be transfigured too, that there will be "a new heaven and earth", a new cosmos.

The biblical idea of the soul is complex and many-stranded. Some of these strands, however, are widely shared. They emphasize that some form of embodiment is proper to such conscious, feeling, willing beings as human persons are. But they refuse to limit embodiment to the precise physical bodies that exist now on this planet. They envisage some form of continuance in which human moral choices for good or evil can be seen and felt with all their implications, and can be worked out to their ultimate conclusion. They give free and responsible moral choice a decisive causal role in the formation of the human future. And they look forward to a final transfiguration of material embodiment that will enable it to become a fully conscious cooperation with and a fully conscious expression of the self-realization of Supreme Spirit in a world of many embodied, unique, and freely acting souls.

Idealist philosophy did not develop independently of such a religious tradition. Both the biblical tradition and the analogous Indian tradition of *Brahman* – one Supreme Self of the cosmos – have been closely interwoven with the growth of philosophical ideas about the nature of reality. Alleged personal experiences of God or of the Supreme Self have for many confirmed the thought that the heart of reality is conscious mind.

Nevertheless, even apart from that, rigorous philosophical thought about the nature of human persons, and about the place of mind in the cosmos, does, in my view, point toward idealism. The argument for idealism stands on its own, and it offers a view of human life that stands in stark opposition to the materialism that characterizes many popularizations of modern scientific thought. It gives human life a value, significance, and purpose of enduring worth. Not only that. It might actually be true.

Notes

Introduction
1. Francis Crick, *The Astonishing Hypothesis*, New York: Simon and Schuster, 1994, p. 3

Chapter One
1. Gilbert Ryle, *The Concept of Mind*, London: Hutchinson, 1949, p. 11
2. *Ibid*, p. 12
3. *Ibid*, p. 15
4. *Ibid*, p. 15
5. *Ibid*, p. 21

Chapter Two
1. Michio Kaku, *Hyperspace*, Oxford: OUP, 1994, p. 15
2. Gilbert Ryle, *op. cit.*, p. 16

Chapter Seven
1. Michio Kaku, *op. cit.*, p. 177

Chapter Nine
1. Malcolm Jeeves and Warren Brown, *Neuroscience, Psychology and Religion*, West Conshohocken, PA: Templeton Press, 2009, p. 52
2. *Ibid*, p. 117
3. John Polkinghorne, *One World*, Oxford: Templeton Foundation Press, 2007, p.102
4. Malcolm Jeeves and Warren Brown, *op. cit.*, p. 49

5. *Ibid*, p. 111

Chapter Eleven
1. Gilbert Ryle, op. cit., p. 61
2. *Ibid*, p. 48
3. *Ibid* p. 47
4. *Ibid*, p. 79

Chapter Twelve
1. *Ibid*, p. 84
2. *Ibid*, p. 110

Chapter Thirteen
1. *Ibid*, p. 167

Chapter Fifteen
1. *Ibid*, p. 62

Short bibliography

I have not given classical texts a publisher, since there are many translations and editions. For them I have given the date of original publication.

Introduction

Francis Crick, *The Astonishing Hypothesis*, New York: Simon and Schuster, 1994.

Gilbert Ryle, *The Concept of Mind*, London: Hutchinson, 1949.

Chapter One

A. J. Ayer, *Language, Truth and Logic*, Harmondsworth: Penguin, 1936.

Ayer's later rejection of logical positivism is expressed in his Gifford lectures, published as *The Central Questions of Philosophy*, London: Weidenfeld and Nicolson, 1973, especially chapter 2.

Rene Descartes, *Meditations on First Philosophy*, especially Meditation 6, second edition, 1642.

Keith Ward, *The God Conclusion*, London: Darton, Longman and Todd, 2009, chapter 3.

Ludwig Wittgenstein, *Philosophical Investigations*, trans. G. E. M. Anscombe, Oxford: Blackwell, 1953.

Chapter Two

George Berkeley, *A Treatise Concerning the Principles of Human Knowledge*, second edition, 1734.

Michio Kaku, *Hyperspace*, Oxford: OUP, 1994.

John Locke, *An Essay Concerning Human Understanding*, book 2, 1690.

A readable, popular account of the interpretation of quantum theory is: Nick Herbert, *Quantum Reality*, New York: Anchor Books, 1985.

For a much more difficult technical account, Paul Dirac, *The Principles of Quantum Mechanics*, Oxford: OUP, 1958.

Short bibliography

And for a selection of "weird" views (where "weird" may well mean "true"), see J. A. Wheeler and W. H. Zureck, *Quantum Theory and Measurement*, Princeton: Princeton University Press, 1983.

Chapter Two
David Hume, *A Treatise on Human Nature*, volume 1, 1739.

Chapter Three
Bernard d'Espagnat, *Veiled Reality*, Reading, MA: Addison-Wesley, 1995.

Immanuel Kant, *Prolegomena to any Future Metaphysics*, 1783. Kant wrote this to explain the "Critique of Pure Reason", and it is in some ways a simpler exposition of his thought.

Keith Ward, *The Development of Kant's View of Ethics*, Oxford: Blackwell, 1972.

Chapter Four
On Hegel, see Stephen Houlgate, *An Introduction to Hegel*, Oxford: Blackwell, 2004.

Keith Ward, *Concepts of God*, Oxford: Oneworld, 1998.

A. N. Whitehead, *Process and Reality*, ed. David Griffin and Donald Sherborne, New York: Macmillan, 1979.

A simpler exposition of Whitehead's thought: John Cobb and David Griffin, *Process Theology; an Introductory Exposition*, Philadelphia: Westminster 1976. Although called theology, there is a lot of philosophy in it.

Chapter Five
Derek Parfit, *Reasons and Persons*, Oxford: Clarendon Press, 1984.

Keith Ward, *Religion and Human Nature*, Oxford: Clarendon Press, 1998.

Bernard Williams, "Personal Identity and Individuation", in *Problems of the Self*, Cambridge: CUP, 1973.

Chapter Seven
Simon Conway-Morris, *Life's Solution*, Cambridge: CUP, 2003.

Chapter Nine
Malcolm Jeeves and Warren Brown, *Neuroscience, Psychology and Religion*, West Conshohocken, PA: Templeton Press, 2009.

Malcolm Jeeves, ed., *From Cells to* Souls – and Beyond, Grand Rapids: Eerdmans, 2004.

For a good account of non-reductive physicalism, see Warren Brown, Nancey Murphy and Newton Malony, *Whatever Happened to the Soul?* Minneapolis: Fortress, 1998.

And for a modern fully dualist account see Richard Swinburne, *The Evolution of the Soul*, Oxford: Clarendon Press, 1986).

Also, Karl Popper and John Eccles, *The Self and its Brain*, London: Routledge and Kegan Paul, 1977.

John Polkinghorne, *One World*, Oxford: Templeton Foundation Press, 2007.

Zombies, stigmergy, and Michel Cabanac can all be found in David McFarland, *Guilty Robots, Happy Dogs*, Oxford: OUP, 2008.

Alvin Plantinga, "Reason and Belief in God" in *Faith and Rationality*, ed. Plantinga and Wolterstorff, Notre Dame, Indiana: University of Notre Dame, 1983.

H. H. Price, *Essays in the Philosophy of Religion*, Oxford: OUP, 1972, especially chapter 6.

A. Quinton, "Spaces and Times", *Philosophy*, volume 37, 1962.

Chapter Ten

David Armstrong, *A Materialist Theory of Mind*, London: Routledge, 1969.

Dan Dennett, *Consciousness Explained*, Harmondsworth: Penguin, 1991.

Benjamin Libet, "Do We Have Free Will?", in *The Volitional Brain*, ed. Libet, Freeman and Sutherland, Thorverton, UK: Imprint Academic, 1999.

Peter Strawson, "Freedom and Resentment" in *Freedom and Resentment and other essays*, London: Methuen, 1974.

Chapter Fourteen

Spinoza, *Ethics*, 1675.

Frank Tipler, *The Physics of Immortality*, New York: Doubleday, 1994.

Chapter Fifteen

Thomas Aquinas, *Summa Theologiae*, Part 1a, question 76.

Aristotle, *De Anima*.

Plato, *Timaeus* and the *Republic*.

Glossary

Absolute idealism   The theory that there is one Absolute Mind of which all finite minds and all matter are parts, or which that Mind generates by inner necessity.

Advaita   One sort of *Vedanta* (see below), claiming that there is in reality only one non-dual Reality of consciousness and bliss, and that the appearance of many souls and things is an illusion.

Antinomies   Kant's word for the contradictions into which, he held, human reason falls when it tries to talk about reality-as-it-is-in-itself.

Basic beliefs   Beliefs that are not based directly on evidence – like the belief that all beliefs must be based on evidence (which is false if there are basic beliefs).

Cartesian dualism   Descartes' view that mind and matter are different substances, and can exist apart. However, as I argue, this view is often misunderstood, since Descartes did not think that they should exist apart.

Common-sense philosophy   The philosophical theory that the world really is just as most people believe it to be, and common-sense beliefs need no rational justification.

Critical idealism   (also called transcendental idealism) Kant's theory that we must assume that reality is ultimately mind-like, but we cannot theoretically demonstrate it, and the material world is not just in our (human) minds.

Critical realism   The theory that objects really do exist apart from us, and we have true knowledge of them. But the way we see them depends upon our special sense-organs and mental apparatus.

Determinism   The theory that every event is wholly determined by some initial state and a set of general laws. So no event could be other than it is.

Dual-aspect idealism   The theory that mind is the ultimate reality, but in the case of human beings, mental events are correlated strongly with physical brain-events, so that a mind can even be called the "brain seen from inside".

Dualism   The belief that humans are made up of two parts, body and mind (or soul). They normally exist together, but can in principle exist apart.

217

"Emergent" universe Universe in which new properties, like consciousness, emerge as matter becomes more complex and organized through time. Such a universe is not just a recycling of properties that have always existed and always will exist.

Epiphenomenalism The theory that minds, consciousness, and mental properties exist, but are wholly caused by brain-events, and have no causal role in the universe.

Evolutionary naturalism The belief that evolution develops by wholly physical laws, without any supernatural or mental influence.

Fatalism The theory that, because determinism is true, there is nothing we can do to change the future. Fate rules!

Holistic explanation An explanation of the parts in terms of the whole of which they are part. For example, you may explain why a cell of the body develops as it does by referring to the whole body of which it is part.

Humanism The view that it is more important to care for human welfare than to practise religious rituals. Historically, many Christians have been humanists, but in modern usage humanism often implies the rejection of belief in God.

Idealism The theory that material objects would not exist without mind or consciousness, so that mind is the primary form of reality, and causes material things to exist.

Intensional state A mental state that refers to something beyond itself. That "something" could be imaginary or fictional, like a character in a novel.

Karma a Sanskrit term referrering to a law of moral reward and retribution, which determines what happens to souls in their different reincarnations.

Logical positivism A philosophical system that is "positive", in that it believes all true assertions must refer to scientifically verifiable facts, and that is "logical", because this is a doctrine about meaning – that factual statements only have meaning if they do refer to such facts.

Materialism The belief that nothing exists except matter – publicly observable things with location in space and time.

Metaphysics A systematic attempt to say what sorts of things exist (minds, bodies, numbers, moral truths, God, etc.), and how they relate to each other. Sometimes called a "world view".

Monism The philosophical theory that there is ultimately only one sort of reality, either spiritual or material, or perhaps have both spiritual or material aspects.

Multiverse The theory that our space–time universe is only one of many such universe, possibly even an infinite number of them.

Naive realism The theory that objects continue to exist just as they appear to us, even when we are not observing them.

Naturalism Usually, the theory that all true statements must refer to "natural" objects – objects subject to physical laws in space and time.

Non-reductive physicalism The belief that materialism (physicalism) is true, but that matter in very complex states (in brains) produces consciousness, which may even have causal power. So minds cannot exist without brains, but they have new, "emergent" properties which simpler forms of matter do not have.

"Open" universe A universe which is not deterministic. The future is open to many possible alternative tracks.

Phenomenalism The theory that nothing really exists except sense-data. Physical objects are logical constructs out of sense-data.

Pluralistic idealism The theory that mind, not matter, is the ultimate reality. But there are many minds, not just one (not just the mind of God, for example).

Primary qualities For Galileo, the qualities that any physical object must possess, whether or not it is observed – properties like position, velocity, and mass, for example.

Process philosophy The metaphysics of A. N. Whitehead, which denies there are enduring substances, but asserts that there is a continuing process of distinct events ("actual occasions") which make up the natural world.

Qualia Immediate objects of the senses, just like sense-data. But there might also be feelings, sensations, and mental images.

Secondary qualities Qualities that only belong to objects when they are observed – like colour and smell. Such qualities are often said to be "in the mind".

Sense-data The things we are immediately aware of by means of our senses – patches of colour, smells, touches, and tastes.

Substance From Aristotelian philosophy, an enduring "thing" which is the bearer of properties (like a tree that remains the same while its leaves grow and die). One continuing substance can have many changing properties.

Teleological explanation Explanation in terms of a goal or purpose, not in terms of general laws that bring some state about. For instance, "I run in order to lose weight" is a teleological explanation.

Vedanta An Indian philosophical system which assumes the truth of the Hindu scriptures (the Vedas and Upanishads), especially that "all is Brahman" [Absolute Mind], and builds various metaphysical systems on that.

Verification principle The rule that all meaningful statements must in principle be capable of being shown to be true by some sense-experiences.

Index of subjects

Index of names

Index of names